Author: Jim Mowatt

Title: From Parkrun To London Marathon

ISBN: 978-0-9956643-1-9

Acknowledgements

Thank you to my lovely wife Carrie, my mum and my brother Tim for all their support.

Thanks also to Richard Panter who guided me as a short-sighted rhino round our local parkruns.

Many thanks to Claire Brialey for her invaluable assistance with getting the the book into a state where I could show it to other people without going into an embarrassing foetal curl.

Thank you also to the parkrun volunteers and all the people who help out and come along to cheer at the London Marathon.

Thank you to the Hitchhiker's Guide To The Galaxy appreciation society, ZZ9 Plural Z Alpha http://zz9.org

I would also like to express a huge thank you to the lovely people at Save The Rhino International.

All photos by Carrie or www.Marathon-Photos.Com

Table Of Contents

Foreword

Why did I decide to put together this book and inflict it upon a world that already has quite a lot of books in it?

The primary reason was that, when I decided to run the London Marathon, I found that the world didn't have enough of the sort of books in it that I wanted to read. I was entranced by the thought of being part of something so magical and wanted to soak up all that delicious anticipation during the months of training that preceded the marathon. The bulk of the anticipation was contained in the training itself, but I was so caught up in the joy of it all that I also wanted to watch videos and read blogs, books, magazines - anything I could find on the subject of the London Marathon. What I most desired was something that would describe what the marathon would look and feel like from the point of view of the runner. My appetite to consume every aspect of this incredible experience was voracious. To decide to run the London Marathon is a step outside the ordinary; to run 26.2 miles is an extraordinary and terrifying thing to do. So I wanted to know how other people had done it. I wanted to know what it would take to do this and what it felt like to run the course. This is my attempt to offer you what I was searching for myself but failed to find in the detail that I required.

I mentioned my primary reason here, but there is also a bit of an ulterior motive lurking around the edges. I chose to run for Save The Rhino and so came to learn more about the work of both this charity and of the other many and varied groups struggling to preserve this magnificent creature. I am donating any money that this book may make entirely to Save The Rhino, in the hope that it will continue to provide a revenue stream (albeit quite probably a very tiny one) to the charity. If you have bought this book then I thank you and Save The Rhino International thanks you too.

Introducing The Journey To The London Marathon

"That last mile is absolutely amazing," she said, "and when you turn to go down the Mall it's the most incredible experience that you could imagine." I did try to imagine it, and reckoned it would be akin to some of the feelings I have previously experienced when I have finished a particularly gruelling run. The actuality was nothing like that: it was a massive emotional assault on a astounding scale.

I shuffled along the Embankment in a world of pain and turned right at the Palace of Westminster. Then I ran along Birdcage Walk, curving around towards the Mall and Buckingham Palace. All the while the noise grew louder and louder, until it became completely unbearable. There was a kind of mass hysteria going on all around me. I'd got a shop to print Jim on my Save The Rhino T-shirt so people could shout out my name and, in a way, join in with my run. What felt like thousands of people were now shouting my name. Faces were looming out of the crowd, telling me that I was awesome or amazing or incredible. It was absolutely terrifying but quite exciting too. My mind couldn't cope with this assault and tried to shut down to get me through. I went with it for a while, but then realised that this was a very special moment and I had to savour it. I forced myself to engage again. I could hear everyone shouting and screaming, all caught up in this amazing event. I zoned in and out as we progressed further down the Mall, trying not to break down and cry with the massive waves of emotion rolling over and around me. At the final turn I saw the finish line and focussed in on that, lurching forward until I crossed the mat with arms held aloft.

It was an incredible day.

So how did I get there?

This is my story, beginning with a first few tentative runs and then switching to my London Marathon story partway through. There will be plenty of info about fundraising, trying to get ready for the marathon and a huge chapter about my marathon experience that is big enough to gobble up all the other chapters and still have room for dessert.

Hope you enjoy it...

My First Run

It all began almost three years earlier when I decided that I would quite like to do a bit of running.

I huffed and puffed my way along the street, feeling terribly despondent, hopelessly fat and desperately unfit. I was getting nowhere fast and this state of being a great big stupid failure wasn't really doing it for me. I was more or less ready to quit. If I could have stopped procrastinating long enough to make the decision I probably would have given up on running almost immediately.

Fortunately I hadn't quite summoned up the energy to get out of my chair and shut the door on this running notion. My friend Richard managed to crowbar in a suggestion through the crack of opportunity left there.

"Why not come down to parkrun on Saturday?" he said.

I could think of many reasons why not to go to parkrun on Saturday, but all of them made me sound rather more whiny and pathetic than I wanted to be. I agreed to go, but warned that I would be diabolically slow.

Running And The Tricksy Brain

I arrived in Milton Country Park for the parkrun that Saturday all prepared to do battle with tiredness, exhaustion and desperate muscle fatigue. What I hadn't realised was that I would also be engaging in a titanic struggle with my mind.

A quick aside here, just to make it clear what parkrun is. Every Saturday morning large groups of volunteers all over the world mark out a five kilometre route, and at 9 am runners turn up to run the course. You get a barcode by registering on the website, and the volunteers will time you and provide a finishing tag. You then take the barcode and finishing tag to the scanning team, and the results are published on the parkrun website. It's a marvellous resource indeed and completely free.

It all sounds so wonderfully easy, but this was five kilometres for goodness sake. That's a long, long way. Surely I, an unfit 50-year-old who hadn't done any running before, could never run that kind of distance? Armed with this mighty multitude of negative thoughts I turned up to give it a try, confident that if I found it too difficult I could just give up and go home. This plan was immediately scuppered when Richard assured me that after he finished he would wait at the finish line to cheer me in.

Damn!

I started near the back of the field and was cheered to find that we set off quite slowly and that the people around me were doing quite a gentle little trot. Excellent, thinks I; this pace will suit me nicely. Unfortunately, even this rather sedate pace was too much for my tired old wreck of a body. After only a kilometre the pain slammed into me as if it was an oncoming truck. I couldn't breathe and my face was contorting madly as I strained desperately to get some air into my lungs. It didn't seem to matter how wide I opened my mouth; I just couldn't get any oxygen in there. I was now swaying from side to side with my mouth agape, doing a fine impersonation of a great galumphing hippopotamus.

My mind screams at me to stop before I die. I keep going. My heart starts thumping and I feel a pain there. See, says my brain; you wouldn't listen to me and now you're going to have a heart attack. I ignore the pain and carry on. Now the muscles in my legs are starting to do strange twanging things. I imagine tendons being stretched to breaking point and snapping abruptly, leaving me with useless floppy limbs. I reject the floppy limbs scenario and keep going. The brain then realises that it needs to get more sneaky if it's going to get me to stop. Maybe you could just rest for a bit, Jim. Surely just a moment's rest wouldn't be too much of a problem. Possibly pausing for a moment might help and then you could run faster after you've recovered. Tempting indeed, but I realise these are brain tricks. At that point one of the volunteers shouts out the time we've been running. I start doing calculations in my head, trying to figure out what speed I'm going and extrapolating my finish time if I actually do finish. This keeps me occupied for some time and I pass the two kilometre marker. This is a revelation as I realise that I haven't died yet and the pain hasn't gotten worse. What's even better is that I'm now breathing fairly evenly. There are still scary wheezing noises emanating from my mouth, but I no longer feel like I'm fighting for every breath. This buoys me up a little and I push on to three kilometres with only muted screaming noises going on inside my head.

Then the doubts come flooding back in. Three kilometres is only a little over halfway. That strange twanging feeling at the back of my knee has returned. Maybe if I keep going it will snap and I may never be able to walk again. I picture myself negotiating the rest of my life in a wheelchair. It all feels so vivid and I'm convinced that the reality will be realised in only a few seconds if I don't stop immediately. I try distracting myself with numbers again but it isn't working. I've slowed down from a trot to a totter and look close to falling over. A volunteer asks me if I'm OK and I try to look brave and assure them that I'm absolutely fine. They ask if I'm sure and I reply in the affirmative. I obviously don't look OK.

Then something magical happens: I encounter the four kilometre sign. This sign means there is just one kilometre left. I start counting down. These are manageable numbers now; the end is no longer an unattainable goal. I count up to a hundred and that means there are only about 900 metres to go. I count to another hundred and think aargh, these numbers aren't going down very much. It's still a long way to the finish. However, suggests my inner monologue, maybe I haven't been entirely accurate and possibly instead of 800 metres left there are only 750. In fact, while I've been thinking about this I could have run another 50 metres so there could only be 700 metres left. No, that's silly; you're just kidding yourself. I argue back and forth about how much I'm deluding myself as regards the distance left to cover and then all doubt is vanquished as I see a sign telling me that there are only 300 metres to go. Hurrah, thinks I, surging forward and then rapidly running out of steam as I find that 300 metres is still quite a long way. Eventually I stagger across the finish line and collect my tag. I lie down on the grass feeling totally exhausted but elated. My mind told me that it couldn't be done. It was absolutely emphatic about it and yet it had lied. I had reached the end and although I ached and hurt, I was not injured and I was now a five kilometre runner (albeit a five kilometre runner who was walking like a drunken cowboy).

This was a distance that I never thought I would attain, and my mind had tried to stop me – but somehow I had managed to push through the negative thoughts and complete the run. Whenever I thought that I could get to the end my brain had insisted forcefully that I was having a whole heap of delusions.

I was not ready to run the London Marathon yet and not even thinking about it. That 5k was just incredibly difficult and, although I felt elated that I had managed to cover that distance, I hadn't got so ambitious that I felt I could go any further. All my running dreams and ambitions over the next few months were centred around trying to improve my 5k parkrun time and improving my fitness. Marathons were for other folks. They were for the kind of people that must have been born with some superhuman gene that set them above ordinary mortals. There was no way that I could ever do anything like that.

Running Is Hard

So, back then after my first 5k I'd found out that running is hard. This is not exactly a revelation. Hundreds of thousands of people all over the world are continually making this discovery. Unfortunately, many of these people find that running is hard and so quit. It's the smart thing to do. If something hurts then it would seem ludicrous to keep doing that thing. If you pricked your finger on a thorn and yelped in pain, would you immediately stick your finger on another thorn? To become a runner you need to be the sort of person who will go back and do it again and again, even though it hurts. In fact you need to accept and appreciate that hurt, because it's the tearing and remaking of your muscles into tools that will enable you to do remarkable things. This is far from intuitive and seems even further from being remotely sensible behaviour.

I think that the key to getting your head around what is happening here is to be able to come to terms with the fact that running is a front-loaded activity. The worst of the pain is either at the very start of running or at the next stage when you move to a greater distance or a significantly faster time. It hurts to begin with, and then it eases and a whole host of much more pleasant feelings come along to keep you company while you run, sprinkling happy dust over you from head to foot. Even when you go out for your regular runs, it can feel unpleasant when you start but there's a point – when your muscles warm up and your breathing becomes a little more even – when it feels like a completely natural thing to do. That's the pay-off here. That's the point when you start feeling the benefit of your training and that you are a proper runner. Your breathing settles down, your legs move smoothly and everything seems to work as it should. You are a runner and your body feels like a well-tuned machine (well, kinda). Of course, this only lasts for a short time until you push it to faster times or greater distances, but it's still a really great feeling and one to be savoured.

I am 52 years old now and I find that it takes quite some time for my muscles to be happy about being engaged in strenuous activity. When I was younger I could just leap into something and the muscles would be very accepting. Yes, we're doing this stupid thing now; that's OK, we'll do it. Now my muscles do much more groaning and grumbling and I need to warm them up and give them a chance to grow accustomed to the fact that what is going to come next will be a trifle uncomfortable. I need about two to three kilometres of gentle running to let them know that something strenuous is going to happen. They whinge, they whine, they creak – but at about two kilometres or so they accept the fact that they are going to have to do some work, albeit occasionally with rather bad grace.

A Lack Of Progress

After my first parkrun I was absolutely exhilarated. I was thrilled that I could do the distance but still rather fearful of it. The tricksy brain thing would happen over and over again. It would whisper to me of my inadequacies and suggest happy strategies for me to just take it easy and maybe try harder another week. I look back on that first year of running and see that I was doing very little outside of parkrun and not even attending that every week. I made steady progress for a short while, but then my times dropped back as I struggled with injury and those whispering doubts.

Remember in that description of my first parkrun that I mentioned a twangy feeling behind the knee. That came along again in future runs and one day at a parkrun did actually do a full twang, to leave me stranded at the side of the track with one foot hovering in the air and looking decidedly tragic. It was during this time that I became aware of all those delightful muscle tears and rips that every runner seems so well acquainted with. What I hadn't yet attained was the awareness of how they happened and what sort of things I should be doing to avoid them. I also wasn't doing enough regular exercise to just leap in and demand things of my legs on a Saturday morning. They reacted badly to these sudden demands and laid me low on several occasions.

This was possibly a time when I might have given up running, but fortunately the parkrun became a bit of a habit. I am naturally an early riser and so, wide awake on a Saturday morning and with the parkrun less than ten minutes' walk away, there seemed to be no reason not to go along.

Increasing The Distance

A year later I was going to parkrun more regularly and starting to feel a little stronger. The injuries were coming along slightly less frequently, and I began to wonder if maybe I could attempt one of the many ten kilometre runs in the area. Richard offered to give me a lift to the Huntingdon race, so the plan was made; I had better do some training.

I started to increase the number of runs that I attempted in a week. It was often just parkrun and one other, but every extra little bit helped.

I would need to train my body to run much further than anything I'd done before. I ran more regularly and found that if I slowed my pace right down I could extend my distance further than 5k. This was a thrilling new discovery. Five kilometres had felt like some kind of ultimate barrier, so breaking it was a surprise and a joy. It was my own tiny world version of breaking the sound barrier or travelling faster than 30mph on a train in 1829. In actuality it was a landmark that passed by rather quietly. My brain didn't melt, my legs didn't fall to pieces, and my toes were all still attached to my feet. Of course, the polar ice caps did do some melting and Queen Elizabeth was admitted to hospital with gastroenteritis – but I sincerely hope that I was not responsible for either of those things.

I was determined to extend my running distance even

further and in one of my training sessions I managed to reach the ten kilometre goal. I ran around the village and then into the country park to do the parkrun route. Around and around the laps I went, breaking down what seemed to be a huge distance into small chunks. I would run the one kilometre lap and then start on the two kilometre lap. Can you manage two kilometres, I would ask myself. Easy, I would answer. 2k is nothing for the mighty athlete you see before you. I would complete the 2k lap and then pose the same question, but this time for the 1k lap. Can you manage a 1k? Toooo easy, lead on. This weird one person question and answer session continued for some time until I checked the app on my phone (Strava) and realised that I had covered nine kilometres and barely noticed any ill effects at all. Of course, the aches and pains then flooded in and I felt as if I could barely move another step. Somehow I did drag my tired and aching frame that extra kilometre and congratulated myself warmly (running is often a very solitary activity, so there is a lot of this internal dialogue going on; it's all perfectly normal, honest. We runners are really all sensible, well balanced individuals). I was now a ten kilometre runner and felt exceptionally pleased with myself.

With all the extra training my 5k times were improving also. I managed to achieve a time that was tantalisingly close to my personal best. Those few seconds teased and taunted me. Next week I would surely beat that time. But wait, next week, the day after parkrun I will be running this fantastically important 10k race. Surely I wouldn't be foolish enough to try to push my running to its limits on the day before such a race?

I think you've probably guessed the answer to this. I was

foolish enough to go for it and injury did ensue. This resulted in my arriving at the Huntingdon 10k with a bit of a limp and feeling rather apprehensive. There was a physio there who I asked to take a look at my leg and advise me on what I should do. He was quite clear on what I should do and that was not to run. Of course I ignored him. I suppose you could say that I was really wasting his time, but I suppose that I was desperately hoping that something could be done that would help me get through the race without any further injury. Possibly there could be some strapping or taping that might assist. It seemed not.

Physiotherapists must get incredibly frustrated with runners; I know I'm not the only one to have ignored the advice of a physio. I've heard from friends who have done this on many occasions. They have set their sights on a goal and are determined to tough it out and carry on. I've since spoken to several physiotherapists and they all seem to have quite a realistic outlook. They know that the best thing for your injury is rest, but they also know it is unlikely that you will stop running. To try to circumvent this they will suggest other activities, such as swimming or resistance training. In fact there are some injuries where you can continue to run, with care. Muscle tears are not among these injuries.

The race began and I set off around the airfield. The pain started to diminish. This was good. This was very good indeed. I could feel that all was not as it should be with my leg, but the pain was minimal and I was moving fairly well. Around the airfield I ran and then off up a gravel path into the fields. I'm running up the hill toward the first water station – and running down the hill, there is the race leader, flying along looking as if he's barely touching the ground. I feel a pang of disappointment that I'm so slow that I am in a position to see this, mixed in with the pleasure of being fortunate enough to have the opportunity to see the leaders cruising by, demonstrating such power and grace. I drink my water and leave these feelings aside for the moment. I have plenty of my own race still to run.

The Huntingdon 10k is a fine course with a considerable amount of variation. After the airfield start, it heads out on gravel paths through a number of fields. Then we are on to quiet country roads until we come to a field of cows. I must admit that cows always worry me a little bit. I know they are usually quite sedate creatures, but they're so huge that I can't help imagining what would happen if they all suddenly started to move at once. Surely they would just plough straight through me, leaving smashed and broken pieces of human strewn around the field. This is not one of my warmer and cuddlier imaginings. The cows did move as we ran across their field but thankfully it was away from us, which is by far the sort of movement that I prefer to see cows get involved in.

On the other side of the field we are into a small suburban housing estate. We wriggle around that and then it's back onto the gravel paths and more fields. I'm in a considerable amount of pain now, but just grit my teeth and push on. My leg is hurting more and there is a limp developing. With only two kilometres to go, though, there's not really any chance I'm going to be stopping. I reach the last water station, grab a cup and then it's down the hill towards the airfield. I now have a strange loping gait as I try to run with only my good leg touching the ground. This is, of course, impossible but the attempt is made nevertheless. I keep running toward the large inflatable arch, but for a long time it doesn't seem to get any closer. This is a long straight road that I'm sure would be a breeze for an aircraft but on my tired and destroyed legs it seems quite endless. I see Richard, Selina and John on my left as I run toward the finish. I hear my name being called out by the announcer and eventually stagger across the finishing timing mat. Someone gives me a plastic bag with various goodies inside, and someone else cuts the timing chip off my shoe.

I am still moving at this point, but as soon as I leave the enclosed semi-circle around the finish my legs collapse under me. I fall to the ground as waves of agony flow through my entire body. I try to stand but just can't manage it. I am wondering how on earth I will manage to get back to my friends. I start to shuffle along using my one good leg, my hands and my bum to achieve some kind of locomotion. My friends start to to wonder why I haven't gone over to join them, so come looking for me. They help me over to the physio tent where he manages not to actually say "I told you so"; he manipulates my leg a little and gives me some ice. The first aider makes a strong suggestion that I should go to hospital but, like a wounded animal, I just want to slink off into a quiet corner somewhere, lie down, and feel sorry for myself. They ask if I think I can get to the car park. I think it unlikely, so the course officials give Richard permission to bring his car onto the airfield. Richard and Selina then drag me out of the tent and bundle me into the car. It must have looked a strange sight with my arm around Richard's shoulders on one side (he's around 5' 10") and Selina's on the other (she's probably less than 5 foot tall and incredibly tiny). Lop-sided as we were, they managed it somehow and got me back home. I spent the next three days unable to stand and just shuffled around the house on my bum. I was the subject of much gentle mockery from my dear, loving wife.

So, I was a ten kilometre runner but had managed to break myself quite badly in the process.

Still a long way from being a marathon runner.

From Watcher To Participant

The London Marathon is the biggest running event of the year for most folks here in the UK, whether we be runners or not. You can mention the London Marathon to almost anyone, from Norwich to Swansea to Aberdeen to Dover, and they will almost certainly feel some sort of cultural connection with you. In Britain we are separated from each other by all manner of cultural thingamabobs and whatchamacallits, but the London Marathon is an event that brings us all together. Even Londoners and non-Londoners feel they might actually be part of the same country for a very short while.

In 2015 I went around to my friend Richard's house to watch the event on the television, and to track other friends around the course using the various rather cool bits of technology that running events now have to record the runners' times and progress. It was great fun but felt just a little bit unsatisfying. Maybe next year I should actually travel down to London and stand at the side of the road cheering people on.

Then the thought occurred: wouldn't it be even better if I were on the course and other people were cheering me on? A most excellent notion. I registered my interest and then later in the year, when the links went live, I signed up to run the London Marathon.

I realised that a lot more people apply than get places in the marathon. Richard has been applying for five years now and has been unsuccessful every time. I am massively pessimistic about most things. If you can imagine a paranoid android (possibly called Marvin) saying in a droning depressed voice, “It will probably be rubbish” or “It will almost certainly fail” then you have my life outlook summed up nicely in an imaginary fictional creature’s simple phrase. This time I was a little more upbeat. I would say out loud that I didn’t expect to get a place, but inside I thought that it was a distinct possibility. Such optimism destabilised me considerably and I was seen smiling on several occasions.

Eventually we reached ballot week and people began to be notified. I checked the letterbox every day, to find nothing but the usual bunch of leaflets from estate agents telling us how much our neighbours have been selling their houses for.

The next week lurched into sight and eventually the notification arrived. It was a magazine that had the word ‘Sorry’ in large friendly letters on the front cover. It said, “Sorry, you have been unsuccessful in gaining a ballot place in the 2016 Virgin Money London Marathon.” This was maybe not so surprising, as more than 247,000 UK residents applied through the ballot for the 2016 marathon. With only about 38,000 people taking part in the run, this meant that well over 200,000 people didn’t get a place through the ballot. The magazine also said something about the possibility of being able to obtain a charity place. I had heard about charity places but didn’t quite understand what that meant. I shall explain it here as I now understand it.

A bunch of charities, it seems, are able to purchase guaranteed marathon places for their organisation, and they then look for people who can guarantee in turn to raise a certain amount of money for their cause. They give the places to these runners and encourage them as much as possible to raise oodles of dosh for the charity and hopefully to boost the profile of the charity too. This is a major televised event after all, so incredibly significant for the charities involved.

I investigated the options and did a few sums. Many charities were asking their runners to raise a minimum of £2,000. I looked at my own finances and tried to imagine how much I could or would give if a running friend asked me to donate to their particular cause. I reckoned that I wouldn't be able to contribute more than about £10. If I asked friends to contribute and they were as skint as me, then I would need 200 people to contribute to get the required £2,000. I figured that it was quite possible that I knew 200 people, but whether I knew them well enough to hit them up for a tenner was another matter altogether. I decided that there was no way that I could raise that kind of money.

What other options might there be to get in on this London Marathon adventure? Well, there is the 'good for age' category. That sounded potentially hopeful in that I'm an old git. I am 52 years old, so I qualify in being aged for these purposes. Unfortunately to qualify properly in this category I would have had to have run less than 3 hours and 20 minutes for a marathon. Having never run a marathon before, this ruled me out immediately.

I had heard that running clubs got guaranteed places in the London Marathon too. Could I get in on a running club place? Well, I wasn't a member of a running club, so that reduced my chances somewhat. I could join a running club, but then why would they give me one of their precious London Marathon places? Maybe I could start my own running club and get a place that way.

To qualify for a club entry place, your club must be affiliated to UK Athletics. If I wanted to form a club, it must affiliate to UKA through English Athletics. It seems there is one London Marathon place for every 1 to 99 members. I only needed one, so all I had to do was to start a club with one member, affiliate to UKA, and I had my place. The affiliation fee was £100 and £13 per athlete. I know, I know. It's a frightfully dodgy idea and perhaps a teensy weensy bit immoral. Those of you worrying about my morality can rest easy that I didn't do this; however, there is the worry that I considered it long enough to research it. There's a list of requirements for any club that wishes to be affiliated to UK Athletics, and I think those requirements should stop anyone from doing anything as downright dodgy as I was considering here.

London Marathon – The Decision To Run For Save The Rhino

I mused for some time over the disappointment of failing to get a ballot place for the London Marathon. I tried to put it behind me, and decided that I would do the Edinburgh Marathon instead and that would be just as good.

The decision stayed like that for some time but then I began reading the 'Sorry' magazine. I saw some of the really great fundraising ideas and thought how much I might enjoy doing some of that stuff. I noticed that one of the charities was Save The Rhino. As a long-time fan of Douglas Adams I have encountered Save The Rhino many times; Douglas, the writer of *The Hitchhiker's Guide to the Galaxy* and *Last Chance to See*, was a founder member of the charity. However, I felt that it was probably too much to take on at the moment, and I was worried about hassling my family and friends to give me donations for the next six months.

It was left like that for a couple of days and then my wife, Carrie, said to me, "You know Save The Rhino is one of the London Marathon charities?"

I said that I was fully cognisant of this.

"Wouldn't you like to run for Save The Rhino?"

Well, of course I would like to, but there were so many potential problems. The main one was that I still thought I wouldn't be able to raise much money. I'd been looking through some of the requirements for other charity places on the marathon and most asked for a £100 registration fee and a pledge to raise at least £2,000. How on earth could I possibly raise £2,000? Carrie waved away my protests. She was buzzing with ideas for raising money and for getting people interested in both the charity and my attempt at running a marathon.

There are times when Carrie gets an idea in her head and at those times she suddenly becomes a nuclear-powered unstoppable train, going downhill with a following wind. She assailed me with so many positive ideas and notions that I was soon swept up in the joy of it all. She was also very cunning with her timing, as I had just completed the Blenheim half-marathon and was quite euphoric about all things running. We were staying at a bed and breakfast place in Woodstock and I was recovering in bed after the run. I had my computer with me and began to browse through the Save The Rhino London Marathon application form. It was only a short step from browsing to starting to fill it out.

Save The Rhino, along with the other London Marathon charities, have only a limited number of places – so they need to make sure they get the best fund-raisers that they possibly can. For Save The Rhino in particular this is their biggest single fundraising event of the year; therefore it is extremely important to make it count. Such thinking is understandable, but it does mean that the application process is rather rigorous, asking lots of desperately searching questions about your motivations and what splendid ideas you have for raising money. The process involves a certain amount of blood, sweat and tears to sell yourself sufficiently that they'll take you on. I wept those tears and sweated that blood for the rest of that day and was still doing so the next day up until kicking out time at the B&B. We decamped to a pub with wifi so that we could finish the application and send it off.

Save The Rhino saw my application and judged that it was good. Only a couple of days later they wrote and offered me a place. I had a few more hoops to jump through, a couple of hurdles to leap and several metaphorical barbed wire fences to crawl under, and I was in.

A London Marathon runner am I.

Now to raise the £2,500 that I promised in my application. This is a terrifyingly large amount of money to ask for from my friends and family. Most of them are struggling through this recession, trying to live frugally and avoid extravagance. I put together my fundraising page and Carrie kicked it off with the first donation. Over the next couple of days more people joined in and after less than a week I found that I was over a fifth of the way toward my target.

This gave me a real boost. I was (and am) incredibly grateful that so many of my family and friends stepped up to give me such a flying start. It made me so much more hopeful that I could achieve my fundraising target for Save The Rhino and possibly even surpass it.

Of course, there was also the small matter of attempting to run 26.22 miles – a distance I'd never run before and a distance that seemed further than my mind could contemplate.

Fundraising

Fundraising both worried and excited me. There were many possibilities, but how on earth would I find the time or energy to get involved in serious fundraising as well as doing the marathon training, holding down a job, and the various other commitments that life kind of insists upon? This would not be easy. Carrie had plans for bake sales (but that would have to be nearer the time if we wanted to capture people's imaginations). I was trying to get people doing a sweepstake to guess my finishing time, but yet again it was many months away from the London Marathon, so people had other things to focus on such as Thanksgiving, Christmas, and a million and one things that would be upon them before Jim decided to trot around London for a bit.

We had several other ideas, many of which I never got around to. I think if I did it again I would definitely put on more events. Maybe a musical concert, a casino, or a comedy night might be good fundraising possibilities. Also, if I staged any of these events in a pub it would get the message out to so many more people and could be a lot of fun. I think I would definitely hold an auction if I did this again. I've done a considerable amount of fundraising in science fiction fan circles for something called the Trans-Atlantic Fan Fund (TAFF). This is a fund that raises money to send fans from Europe to North America and from North America to Europe, to promote the connections between fan groups across those continents. I was the beneficiary of the fund in 2013 and visited Toronto, Abingdon, Seattle, Santa Cruz, San Francisco, Las Vegas, the SF Worldcon in San Antonio, and New Orleans before coming back home. I've held quite a large number of auctions for TAFF; they always create a buzz and raise the bulk of the money to support the fund.

I asked several people for advice on fundraising and they mostly said similar things about being passionate and ensuring that you actually get out there and ask for donations. Yvette Keller, who has had some considerable fundraising experience, had lots of good advice. One of the most useful points for me was the rule of seven. Apparently, unless people specifically say no when you ask, you should keep asking again using various different avenues. You can ask using Facebook, emails, face-to-face communication and so on, up to seven times, to give them plenty of opportunity to donate. Yvette tells me that most people will want to donate if they can, but life all too often intervenes and they don't get around to it unless you remind them. I probably didn't approach anyone anywhere near seven times, but knowing this 'rule' existed did give me the confidence to ask rather more than I would have otherwise.

After the initial flurry of contributions from friends and family, donations were beginning to stall. At this stage I remembered something that I'd mentioned in my application to run for Save The Rhino. I had suggested that I borrow their rhino suit to do some shorter runs before the marathon and hopefully raise some money that way. Of course, this meant going to London to collect the suit and then trying to get it home on public transport: quite a challenge.

Collecting The Rhino Suit

I picked up the suit from the offices of Save The Rhino on 30th November and then had the wonderfully bizarre experience of trying to get it back to Cambridge on public transport. Fortunately everyone we encountered was absolutely wonderful and splendidly helpful.

The Save The Rhino office is at 217 Long Lane in London. It looks like so many other offices, having lines of computers with people sat there typing away or trying to outstare a computer screen. What makes this place a little different is that it is strewn with very large rhino costumes. I don't think I had fully appreciated just how big these costumes were before I got up close to them. In this fairly small office the huge rhino costumes were actually quite intimidating. It took several minutes before I had properly grown accustomed to their presence.

The costumes have now become an iconic part of the London Marathon and they tend to crop up in all sorts of other weird and wonderful fundraising events, including a climb up Mount Kilimanjaro (then worn by Douglas Adams) and epic races such as the Marathon des Sables and Comrades. They originated in a musical called *Born Again*, designed by Gerald Scarfe and built by Niki Lyons. Save The Rhino asked if they could have them when the show was over and have been making good use of them ever since.

We were sat at a desk and Grace Dibden had me fill out

some forms where I promised to hand over oodles of cash if I lost or damaged the costume. This was a little bit daunting, but it kind of made sense; this is a relatively small charity and they rely quite heavily upon these costumes to help them raise money.

Grace plied us with cups of tea while she asked questions about my fundraising and training. I then tried on the rhino outfit and took it out into the courtyard for a bit of a run around. Carrie took some video with her phone and much fun and giggles were had.

Eventually it was time to go. Rather nervously I donned the costume and headed out of the courtyard to begin the journey home.

Walking back to Borough tube station we were tooted many times by passing traffic, and were then ushered through the turnstiles by the lovely folks at the station. They asked me to do a bit of posing as they took pictures with their phones to show what sort of people they had to deal with every day. Somewhat dazzled by all the attention, I was only too happy to be photographed by the people on the turnstiles. Gosh! I'm a rhino superstar.

I couldn't stand up straight on the tube train and spent most of my time bent over trying not to get in the way of people boarding and alighting the train. I heard someone say to Carrie, "He could sit over here." She thanked them but said, "I don't think it's possible for him to sit down."

We lurched out at Kings Cross, tottered into the station and found ourselves a homebound train. Thankfully we had got onto the train before rush hour, and so managed to find a place where I could unlatch myself from the rhino costume and drape it across several seats.

We had wondered about catching a bus from Cambridge train station but, having now witnessed the sheer size of this rhino costume, we realised that it just had to be a taxi. We were asked searching questions in the queue about the costume. These are the same questions I have been asked every time I wear the rhino suit, so I shall try to answer them here to satisfy your curiousity:

How heavy is it?

Not very heavy. It's only about 10 kilogrammes, but it is frightfully awkward and bounces about everywhere.

Is it really difficult to get in and out of?

Not as difficult as you might think. It's got a rucksack structure inside it, so you just need to strap it on.

Can you see out of it?

Not very well. I have no peripheral vision; I just see a porthole in front of me and so rely quite heavily on people with me to make sure I don't veer left or right in front of other folk.

Do you think you can run a marathon in it?

Currently, no. I don't have the strength or stamina to run 26 miles in this contraption. I dearly wish that I could, but fortunately there are many people who can run a marathon in the costume and they come back year after year to raise money for Save The Rhino.

We got into a taxi with some difficulty. We put the head in the boot and the costume in the back seat. It entirely filled up the space there and I slid underneath it. I suspect the driver wasn't entirely pleased that the spikes the rhino head slides onto were digging into his roof. But I'm pretty sure that they didn't do any damage.

The rhino suit is now filling up our spare bedroom. No visitors, I'm afraid, until the rhino has left the building.The cats were downright terrified of that room.

Fundraising As A Rhino

So now I had the suit home I should put it to use. I wondered about doing some kind of endurance event, maybe on a treadmill, maybe in the lobby of a supermarket or at the front of a civic building; it struck me that a rhino on a treadmill would attract a great deal of attention. I still think it would, but I decided instead to combine my love of parkrun tourism with fundraising for Save The Rhino. Carrie and I often head north for Christmas and New Year, to stay with my mum in Yorkshire and Carrie's mum in Scotland. We could tour several parkruns and hopefully raise some money.

I trawled the contact pages for the parkruns that I wished to visit, to check that they were OK with me coming along and what might be allowed as regards fundraising. It was much as I expected with most of them, in that they were happy for me to come along to the run. Raising the profile for Save The Rhino was also fine, but maybe I should avoid shaking collecting tins under people's noses. This seemed fair enough. If they allowed me to hassle people to donate then it could set a precedent, and every Saturday at parkruns would become an obstacle course of good causes making you feel guilty because you can't give to them all.

I agreed a strategy with the various run directors where I would run in the suit and give out cards to anyone who approached me; these cards would give details of where people could donate. This might seem a bit limiting, but if you are wearing a rhino suit then almost everyone approaches you and some of them offer real cash money too.

I did eight rhino parkruns, at Cambridge, Huntingdon, Wimpole, Ayr, Eglinton, Woodhouse Moor, Temple Newsam, and Oakwell Hall. It was a fantastically enjoyable, although at times logistically difficult, rhino tour. I'll relate the tales of a couple of those rhino runs here and you can find the rest at my running blog, http://abitofrunning.com/

Cambridge Parkrun: The First Rhino Run

It was a frightfully windy day on 5th December in a small village on the periphery of Cambridge. People were converging on Milton Country Park for the weekly 5k parkrun.

A large grey creature stepped out onto the street and wobbled a little as it tried to figure out where the footpath was. The ever helpful Carrie stepped in front and the rhino followed along. Cars stopped in the street, dogs barked, and people stared as we staggered onwards.

We arrived at around 8.30 am and the photographer from Cambridge News, who I had emailed earlier in the week, was already there. He waved and pointed and we all moved this way and that to the rhythm of the media. Various parkrun volunteers were ushered across to join in, and a queue of people formed up to have their picture taken with the rhino. Having no peripheral vision and not being able to hear too much, I just stood there most of the time, imprisoned within the confines of my suit, as things happened around me.

Carrie was busy handing out cards with the web address of the fundraising site and offering people stickers with the logo for Save The Rhino. The kids, in particular, seemed to like the stickers. Several people gave us their coffee money and on behalf of the rhino we were happy to accept.

We set off at 9 am and I shuffled after the crowd. I was moving well but had no idea where I was putting my feet. I stumbled several times over puddles, holes, and even a small pebble.

The noise inside my suit was incredible. The whole thing was bouncing about and all I could hear was swishing and swooshing and banging and crashing. Richard was running beside me and trying to keep up the conversation. I yelled back as best I could. I suspect I misheard most of what he said and it's quite possible that most of my responses made no sense at all. Nice chap that he is, though, he made no mention of this and still struggled valiantly to chat and guide me along as we ran through the park.

We started slowly but increased the pace as we went along. An ache developed in my back, probably brought on by having to bend forward to peer out of the suit. As our pace increased we started to pass people and made several of them (especially the ones wearing headphones) jump and utter little shrieks of panic. Evil rhino that I am, I found this immensely satisfying.

It was an incredibly difficult run. I got hotter and hotter inside the costume and was nicely stewed by the end. I staggered over the line feeling enormously relieved to get there without keeling over and becoming a stranded rhino in a puddle in the park. Various people suggested that I try to run the marathon in the rhino suit. After this outing I could confidently say that I haven't the strength or the stamina to do it. (It was possible that I might have gained that stamina and strength with my winter training, but very unlikely.)

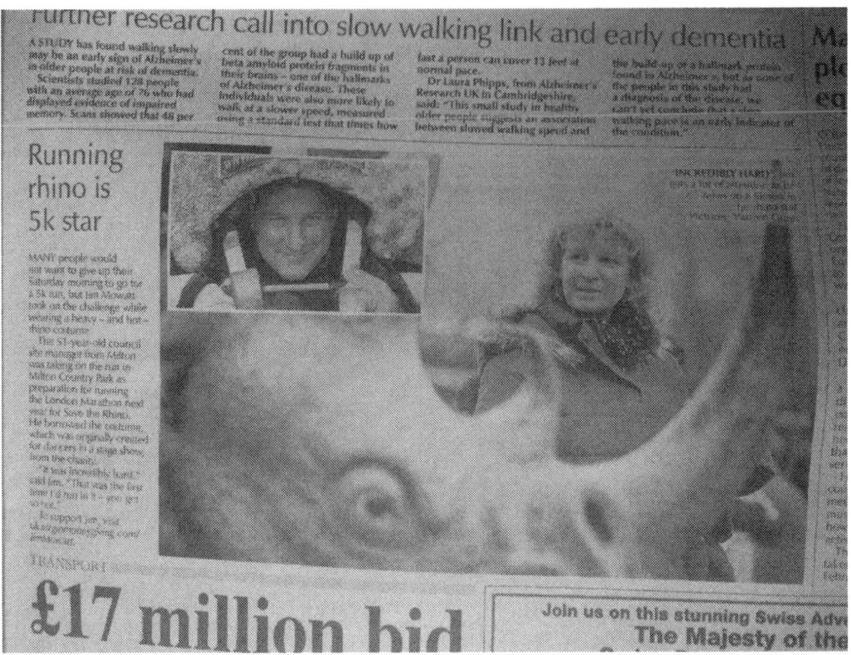

Further research call into slow walking link and early dementia

A STUDY has found walking slowly may be an early sign of Alzheimer's in older people at risk of dementia.

Scientists studied 128 people with an average age of 76 who had displayed evidence of impaired memory. Scans showed that 48 per cent of the group had a build up of beta amyloid protein fragments in their brains – one of the hallmarks of Alzheimer's disease. These individuals were also more likely to walk at a slower speed, measured using a standard test that times how fast a person can cover 13 feet at normal pace.

Dr Laura Phipps, from Alzheimer's Research UK in Cambridgeshire, said: "This small study in healthy older people suggests an association between slowed walking speed and the build-up of a hallmark protein found in Alzheimer's, but as none of the people in this study had a diagnosis of the disease, we can't yet conclude that a slow walking pace is an early indicator of the condition."

Running rhino is 5k star

MANY people would not want to give up their Saturday morning to go for a 5k run, but Jim Mowatt took on the challenge while wearing a heavy – and hot – rhino costume.

The 51-year-old council site manager from Milton was taking on the run in Milton Country Park as preparation for running the London Marathon next year for Save the Rhino. He borrowed the costume, which was originally created for dancers in a stage show, from the charity.

"It was incredibly hard," said Jim. "That was the first time I'd run in it – you get so hot."

TRANSPORT

£17 million bid

Join us on this stunning Swiss Adv

The Majesty of the

Cambridge News rang me for an interview and they got a whole bunch of photos for the paper, so maybe we got a few more donations from that (checking later, I'm not sure that we did get any more donations as a result of the newspaper story).

It was an enjoyable day. Cambridge parkrun and my fellow parkrunners were all splendidly supportive. My friends Lloyd, Steve and Richard all helped and it was great to have them around. Run director Paul Beastall was really great, and of course my wonderful wife, Carrie, ensured that I was organised and handed out stickers and contact cards to anyone who wanted one. She also made sure that I didn't get run over on the way to and from the parkrun, for which I was most grateful.

Most excellent fun!

A Little Parkrun History

You may have noticed that parkrun has received many mentions in this narrative. I gave a brief description of what it is, way back when I was telling the tale of my first parkrun. However, this movement has become such an incredible phenomenon that I'd like to let you know a little bit about how it all started.

It all began, appropriately enough, in a park. This was Bushy Park in Surrey and the event was known as the Bushy Park Time Trial. The date was 2nd October 2004 and thirteen people ran a measured five kilometre distance around the park. The event was repeated every Saturday for the next two years and over that time the number of people who went along to run increased considerably. This was rather a surprise - but even more of a surprise was the type of people who were taking part. There was an expectation that club runners would attend, but people were bringing along partners and children. It was becoming a time trial for people of vastly varying abilities and a social experience too. There were increasing demands for similar events elsewhere, and in 2007 the second Time Trial began on Wimbledon Common. Richmond and Banstead soon followed, and then it broke out of London to pop up in Leeds.

Leeds was quite an interesting addition to the parkrun family. It was started by Tom Williams, who was working in the Sports and Exercise Science Department at the University of Leeds. He had read about the Bushy Park Time Trial in *Runner's World* and took the concept to his university department, who at the time were looking for ways in which their students could engage with the local community through volunteering and physical activity. They were enthusiastic about the idea and Tom got in contact with the principal mover behind parkrun, Paul Sinton-Hewitt. Paul immediately offered huge amounts of assistance with equipment and software, and the Hyde Park Time Trial on Woodhouse Moor was born. Tom incorporated the event into the curriculum for his department and the students became regular volunteers at the event, making it a part of their Sports and Exercise studies.

Parkrun is now a global phenomenon, taking place in twelve different countries around the world. Currently, in 2016, 780 runs take place every week with around half a million runners.

The recipe for the success of parkrun probably lies with its simplicity. All a runner has to do is register on the website, print off their barcode, and then take that barcode to one of the events. The barcode and finish token are scanned at the end, and only a few hours later all the results appear on the parkrun websites. Obviously lots of volunteers put in huge amounts of effort to make this happen, but for the runner the process is all incredibly simple and free. As you've seen from my early chapters, beginning to run is a difficult process and it's hard enough fighting your own body and brain to overcome those initial trials. If there were more barriers - such as a financial commitment, a complicated process or having to achieve a particular standard before being allowed to take part - then it would be all too easy to quit.

I often wonder whether I would have continued running if there wasn't the incentive of attending parkrun on a Saturday morning.

So that's my potted history of parkrun (small p, you'll have noticed; they insist upon it, though I know not why). Let's get back to the story of my parkrun rhino.

Two Parkruns In One Day

I'm visiting my mum in Leeds and there are parkruns on New Year's Day. Of course I have to go. What's more, I want to do two parkruns in one morning. Also, I want to do them in rhino costume. All sounds perfectly reasonable to me.

Carrie sighs and agrees to come along. I can see so little out of the front of the rhino suit that I need as much assistance as I can possibly get just to make sure I arrive on the start line. Therefore I'm really grateful that she can come along to help.

There's a fine gathering on the moor. As with last year, there seems to be a tradition of gathering near the finish funnel and then moving back to the start for the pre-run briefing. Sam, the run director, does the briefing. He mentions someone who got what sounded like about 84 per cent in age grading and also someone doing their 250th parkrun. Unfortunately I can't hear much from inside the rhino, but many congratulations to them. Sam also does a wonderful shout-out for me and talks a little about the sorry plight of the rhino.

The run director counts us down and then sends us on our way around the course. It's a nice flat course, although there are occasional patches of ice. We do a fair amount of looping around and pass some places three times during the run. It's not the most scenic parkrun I've ever done, but it's an excellent example of being able to put on a fine run even in quite a limited space. They've really used what they have in an interesting way, alternating the loops slightly each time around. I follow someone in an orange T-shirt for a while and eventually manage to pass by. Then I follow someone in a 250 shirt, but I don't have enough energy to pass her and she leaves me staggering along behind. It looks a really nice shirt. Hope they're still doing them when I get to 250 parkruns.

I hauled myself across the finish line and run director Sam came across for a chat. I thanked him for the shout-out at the start and we had a photo taken together. Sam then grabbed my finish token and barcode and scanned them in for me, and shooed me away to my next parkrun at Temple Newsam, asking me to remember him to Ronnie who would be run directing there.

Later I received my Woodhouse Moor parkrun time and it was a new rhino personal best:

"Woodhouse Moor parkrun results for event #435. Your time was 00:32:49."

We rush to the car and I stuff the rhino head into the boot, with the body of the suit draped across the back seat. Other people are also heading for the next parkrun and there is soon a convoy of parkrunner cars heading across Leeds toward Temple Newsam. We arrive, park the car, and trot down to the start, passing the grand Elizabethan stately home that is Temple Newsam House. There are many glorious settings all around the world for parkruns but I imagine few could compete with Temple Newsam for sheer grandeur.

Goodness!

There are a lot of people here at Temple Newsam.

The run director is doing the pre-run briefing but I can't hear any of the words. I'm not sure the people around me can either. My guess is that there may be rather more people here today than they are accustomed to. However, it all seems really well-organised, so they've handled the large turnout really well.

Jill pops over to say hello. She's been answering my email enquiries about the parkrun. Hiya Jill, good to see you.

Dogs are barking at me and I'm meeting folk I saw at Woodhouse Moor. I'm also seeing a lot more children at this parkrun and they are all intensely curious. That gives us a great opportunity to offer them Save The Rhino stickers and talk to them and their parents a little about the endangered rhino. I see a family running with a buggy and a small dog. They have a GoPro Hero strapped to one of the buggy arms and assure me they have footage of the rhino from Woodhouse Moor. I wish I'd swapped email addresses with them to ask for some of that footage. Quite apart from gathering more rhino video, I would like to see how the Hero performs; I quite fancy getting one for myself.

(He did contact me through my website and had some wonderful footage from the GoPro; thank you, Martyn Lewis of Martyn Lewis Photography in Leeds: http://www.martynlewisphotography.com/)

We set off past the glorious Elizabethan mansion and out through the formal gardens. Down the long hill we go and people pass me here who I'd met at Woodhouse Moor. They say hello and cheer me on and then someone starts chatting to me about the run I am due to do tomorrow at Oakwell Hall. It seems he is the chap I was emailing to notify that I would be there. He wishes me luck, says that he looks forward to seeing me tomorrow, and moves on.

We continue down the hill and I try out the hill running strategy that I developed when I ran the Blenheim half-marathon. I have found that if I do shorter strides and turn my legs over faster on downhill stretches then it seems to put a little less pressure on my quads and makes me go slightly faster. We reach the bottom of the hill, turn left at the motorway (the least pretty bit of the Temple Newsam grounds), and curl back along the edge of the woods until we are once again struggling up the hill toward the house. Twice around we go and the second time we are curved around the hill a little until we burst out into the finish funnel.

I queue to be scanned behind the girl in the orange T-shirt. I'd finished before her at Woodhouse Moor but she was really pleased to finish in front of me here at Temple Newsam. "I couldn't be beaten by a rhino twice in one day," she said.

I was going to get a coffee afterwards, but there was a very long queue and I had more family duties to attend to at my mother's house in Tingley. We made our way back up by the house and stopped for a moment outside the glorious front doors for just one more picture. We were immediately pounced on by large numbers of people asking if we'd let them take a picture of their child standing by the rhino. It was really sweet and I posed for many photos beside children who were either delighted or terrified to take part in a rhino photo. I also discovered that there was an extra incentive to have your picture taken with a rhino here. The rhino is the animal of the Leeds rugby league team, Leeds Rhinos, so a more popular beastie in that city than you might expect.

Arriving back in Cambridge after the Christmas and New Year tour of northern relatives and parkruns, I took stock of how we'd done. I had to admit that in fundraising terms it wasn't a raging success, but it had added money to the total that I wouldn't have got otherwise and also had been a lot of fun.

I had also now had quite a bit of experience running in the rhino costume. For any future rhino runners here are my top five tips:

If possible, practise running in your rhino costume before the main run.

This will bring to light all manner of awfulness such as how dogs respond to you (some were terrified; some wanted to get inside the suit with me), and where the costume rubs, chafes, and generally mashes up tender bits of your body.

If possible, find a friend as seeing eye.

The rhino costume gives you a very restricted view. If a friend can help prevent you ploughing through the crowd and causing a major incident then this will probably be a 'good thing'.

Put tape and lube over chafing bits.

If you find that bits start to chafe over short distances, then it is possible that they will rub away entire limbs before you finish. Take precautions.

Recruit a friend with a collecting tin.

The rhino costume doesn't have pockets. If you're raising money for something, then make sure there is someone around who can stash any cash that may be proffered/thrown in your direction.

Adapt your costume.

If you do manage to practise with your costume then you will discover all sorts of problems. One of the ones I found with the rhino costume was this cutesy little tail thing it had. It looked really sweet in videos from behind. However, it kept tapping me on the leg and made me want to massacre everyone within a five mile radius after only about five minutes. I managed to tuck it up and then tape it out of the way. It meant that my costume lost a little cuteness, but fewer people were horribly murdered than would have been otherwise.

Now, how else can I use this costume to raise money and awareness for Save The Rhino?

Rhino Need Gait Analysis Too

There were strange happenings in Cambridge on Thursday night. A rhino shone his torch into a pay and display machine to see how hungry the machine might be. It was hungry indeed, but this was a rhino with a pocketful of change and he wasn't afraid to use it.

Parking machine paid for, Richard guides me across the road and into the Anglia Ruskin Building. We cause a stir as we enter the building and I'm not even wearing my head. Richard is casually carrying this head in one hand while greeting people with the other. Suddenly people are pulling cameras from everywhere. I reckon it's not really my face they are after, so dutifully don the rhino head.

We get chatting to a few folk and we are talking about running shoes. This is an event featuring Saucony, after all, and running footwear is what they do. What they are doing here is showing off their shoes to runners. Tempted as I am by their shoes, I am even more excited by the whizzy new gait analysis machine they told me about. It's got lots of cameras and super techie features that will help me figure out what my feet are doing when I run and, I hope, give me a clue as to the sort of shoe that would fit my running style. Saucony were keen for me to come along, but especially keen if I were to bring the rhino suit. Soon after I arrived, they plonked me onto the treadmill and set me going. I bumbled along and soon got into a steady rhythm. I could hear strange shrieks and bizarre exhalations of air as folk wandered into the room and beheld the sight of a rhino on a treadmill. I ignored it all and just kept plodding away. It's just another day on the treadmill, having my rhino running gait analysed.

The machine stops doing what it does and we go to view the computer to see what it shows. It's absolutely fascinating zooming in on my legs, running the video backwards and forwards to see how my foot lands and what shenanigans it may get up to as it progresses onwards to the next stride.

So what did it show, this machine of wonder? Well, you might (or might not) be surprised to hear that it showed I needed new running shoes. My right foot was collapsing inwards as it landed. The technician was able to display in fine detail how my foot rolled on to the inside. It did look very bad for me as it threw my posture sideways and therefore, I imagine, could cause all manner of injury.

A fascinating machine, and if its primary purpose was to help sell shoes then it did its job. I went along to Up And Running a few days later and purchased a fine pair of Saucony Triumph ISO running shoes. he shoes felt absolutely wonderful. I actually did feel like I had a spring in my step. Surely with such excellent footwear this marathon will be a breeze.

Running Books

When I decided to write this book, my principal motivation was that there weren't enough books about running to satisfy my hunger for the subject, particularly my desire to know more about training for and running the London Marathon. I also wanted to know as much as possible about fundraising, to give me the confidence to raise the £2,500 that I had promised I would raise for Save The Rhino. This doesn't mean that there weren't any relevant books, but just that there weren't enough to satiate my need for information and immerse myself in the process. There are several books about unfit people such as myself embarking upon the long trek to being marathon-ready and also some brilliant books about running in general.

Books about running aren't always easy to find, though, so here's my quick guide to the best of the bunch.

General Running Books

1. *Born To Run* by Christopher McDougall. This is my favourite running book and is massively inspirational as well as being an exhilarating story. Christopher is continually nagged by running injuries and wonders why such injuries are so prevalent among runners. His journey to discover the answer takes him to Copper Canyon in Mexico where he encounters a running people known as the Tarahumara. Running is part of their culture and injury seems much rarer among this tribe than we

would expect. Christopher ponders many theories and wonders whether barefoot running may be the answer. Could it be that humans are specifically designed to run, and that if the foot is allowed to flex and move as it touches the ground then it will strengthen and so encourage good running form? His voyage of discovery takes him through the story of Nike and the invention of the waffle iron sole to scientists researching the theory that humans evolved through persistence hunting. He also takes a group of runners (including one of the biggest ultra-running names, Scott Jurek) into the canyons to compete against the Tarahumara. I have read this book many times and absolutely adore it.

2. *Running With The Kenyans* by Adharanand Finn. Without a doubt the Kenyans dominate the world of marathon running. Adharanand takes his family out to stay in a small town in Kenya to train with the cream of the Kenyan runners and try to find out why they are so good. A wonderfully immersive book that goes beyond the nuts and bolts of running to also give some fascinating insights into some of the athletes' motivations.

3. *Ultramarathon Man: Confessions Of An All Night Runner* by Dean Karnazes. Dean was out with a bunch of friends celebrating his 30th birthday. The realisation that he had reached the age of 30 was something of a shock to him. He was feeling as if there was something important that was missing from his life. He excused himself to go to the toilet but then kept going out into the night air and began to run. He ran all night and in the morning stopped at a payphone to call his wife and ask if

she could come to collect him. He was 30 miles away, absolutely exhausted, but emerged from the experience having gained a great deal of mental clarity. Dean went on to become a fantastically inspirational ultra-runner and also a pretty good writer.

London Marathon Books

1. *Fat Guy Runs A Marathon* by Terry Lander. This is a book that had much of what I craved when looking for memoirs of training for and running the London Marathon. Terry begins his journey as an overweight chap clawing desperately along the path to marathon readiness, and finishes as a less overweight chap who has run the London Marathon. Along the way he gives us a wonderfully comic insight into the trials and tribulations of managing to squeeze in the training required to take on such a massive challenge. He also keeps us amused and entertained throughout. I do wish there had been more detail of the marathon itself, though.

2. *It's Just Four Times Round The Village* by Helen Stothard. I got more of the London Marathon experience from this book. Helen details a very large number of runs leading up to the London Marathon, and then spends a significant chunk of the book telling the story of her marathon run. It gave me a real feeling of the experience and also considerable encouragement that I could do it too.

3. *Running Like A Girl* by Alexandra Heminsley. This

book details Alexandra's training for and running the London Marathon *twice.* It is a splendidly whimsical book and contains a lot of the detail that I would have liked to read before the London Marathon. Unfortunately the publisher's description seemed to emphasise how much it was focussed upon female runners, and that kind of pushed me away. I was convinced that there would be huge chunks of the book devoted to bra engineering, wobbly bums and breasts, and maybe some stuff about childbearing just to emphasise that this is stuff that is just for girls. Fortunately it is not as exclusionary as I had feared. It is a fine book and will tell you a lot about training for and running the London Marathon. The second half talks about the first women to run in marathons. This does have some interesting information in it, but we lose the personal connection there that Alexandra does so well in the first half of the book.

4. *Breaking The Wall* by S R Boulton. This is a slightly different creature to the books I've mentioned before: it is a work of fiction that takes us on three separate journeys toward the London Marathon. Jake, Harry and Teresa have huge mountains of despair and anguish to wade through just to get to the start line of their training, never mind the marathon. This book lingers a little longer over the race, giving me a bit of a feel for the London Marathon long before I got there. I liked some of the little details such as there being 81 pubs on the route; I did wonder about trying to count them during the run but on the day I was so overwhelmed with emotion that I wasn't really up to anything as analytical as counting.

Training For The Marathon

As soon as I decided that I was going to run it, I sucked up as much information as I possibly could about the London Marathon, marathons in general, and training for the distance. There was absolutely no shortage of advice about training. Week by week they would chart out how many miles you should be doing and at what sort of intensity. What a good idea, I thought. Free advice from people who definitely seem to know what they are talking about. I would be a complete fool to ignore this.

I ignored it.

My training was a strange hodgepodge of trying to grab bits of running time during the week and then a glorious long slow run on a Sunday morning. I tried running to and from work for a while. This really helped me increase my mileage but logistically was quite complicated, arranging what clothes or what kit I could keep at work and always trying to remember where my towel was.

There was also the Wednesday night social run from the running shop, Up And Running, on Trinity Street in Cambridge. A group of us would meet at 6pm at the shop and do a 10k run around different parts of Cambridge. At first I found these rather difficult. They were aimed at a pace which would be reasonably gentle/social for most of the runners but it was a trifle fast for a slow plodder such as myself. They were happy to wait for me as I huffed and puffed along behind the pack, but I stopped going for a while as I just felt too embarrassed at holding them all back. Later, as the months passed and I increased my speed and endurance, I returned and could run and chat with the rest of them. It was a good feeling and that sense of progress gave me such a boost. I grabbed all the boosting I could. Somewhere in my future there was a marathon to run and I needed all the confidence I could get.

Although I say that I ignored the many training schedules published all over the internet, I reckon that I probably adhered in a very loose fashion to some of them. The basic pattern seems to be to do long runs at the weekends and try to run three times during the week. This leaves two days rest each week. There's lots more detail, including some horrendous-sounding thing known as intervals or even fartleks. There is also a really useful rule which I ignored (can you spot a pattern here?) about how much you increase your distance each week. The rule is not to increase your distance by more than 10 per cent. I went from 40 kilometres in one week to 75 the next. A hamstring injury ensued and almost scuppered my marathon. Hopefully anyone out there reading this will be a damn sight smarter than I.

I learned quite a few things during my training, mostly by making mistakes and suffering from them. I learned (too late) not to increase my distance too quickly, but I also learned a bit about how to keep myself hydrated and fuelled during the run.

I needed to drink but hated carrying anything. Therefore

those funky little hand-held bottles were no use to me at all. I decided to try a hydration pack. This is a small rucksack that holds a plastic bladder inside. There is a tube which comes out of the top, and the idea is that you can slip this into your mouth and take a sip whenever you feel the need. It sounds a great idea, but I must have done something wrong with it as a leak developed and I ended up with the water all over my back and very little left for drinking. I then tried a gunslinger's holster type thing and this works beautifully. It only holds about a litre of water but that just about gets me through long runs. I also bought a phone holder to strap to my arm and a small elasticated bag to go around my waist (for keys and emergency cash), and so carrying things in my hand became a thing of the past.

There was an incident locally where a runner collapsed and died near the local country park and this encouraged me to purchase a parkrun wristband which had their barcode on it plus an emergency contact telephone number. Hopefully if I topple over somewhere, then some helpful soul will call the number wrapped around my wrist so that folks will know where I am.

Embarrassing chafing was often a problem on my long runs. My whole body would sweat quite alarmingly and all that water needed somewhere to go. Gravity did its thing and it all travelled downwards. Unfortunately this meant that an awful lot of it ended up in my pants. This was more than a little unpleasant and led to some ouch moments as I lowered myself into the bath after a run. I had a look at my running shorts and noticed that they had an internal lining of their own; maybe I didn't actually need to wear underpants underneath these shorts. I've since taken to running without undies and the chafing is much reduced.

My favourite run of the week was the long slow run on a Sunday. This involved me going out quite early on Sunday morning and just running around for a bit. I would choose a direction and have a sort of general plan about where I might go. There was a real joy in taking the opportunity to explore and soak up some of the beauty of this delightful city (Cambridge) in which I live. I would be running along and see some tree-lined passageway leading away from the road. I would veer off down this and manage to get myself splendidly lost. I would wind around and around and eventually encounter a sign that would point me back toward my general and rather unfocussed route plan.

I've been asked many times why I run or what I want to get from all this training. Obviously the London Marathon was a goal, but a longer-term goal is to maintain the strength and fitness to continue these long slow runs and possibly make them even longer. I would like to be able to set off at 7 in the morning and run all day to see where I could get to in the evening. I think that would be a grand adventure. In the next chapter I shall describe one of my long Sunday runs before the marathon, to try to give you some insight into the anarchic rambling nature of it.

A Long Slow Run

I always try to get in a fairly long run if I possibly can on a Sunday morning. If I get up early I can be out and back before my wife even begins to stir.

This morning, however, I was out for some considerable time and she had already stirred and then begun to wonder if I was lying in a ditch somewhere with my life's blood oozing out onto the abundant vegetation that surrounded and encased my defenceless body.

The truth was somewhat more prosaic.

I had set off without any kind of plan and then just kept going. I got lost several times but ended up covering what, for me, was a very long distance (25km). It's given me real hope that, with training, I may be able to reach the marathon distance.

I began my run just weaving around Milton Country Park, trying to figure out where I was going next. My first thought was the busway. This is a nice long straight piece of tarmac that's really easy to run on. It was tempting but I decided against it in favour of something that might be a bit more of an adventure.

I broke out of the Country Park and headed toward the river. First decision there: should I turn left toward

Clayhithe, or right and over Baits Bite Lock? I chose the latter and over the river I went, heading straight on through the field, over a tiny wooden bridge that made me think of Billy Goats Gruff and Trolls, and then up to Horningsea.

In Horningsea I found a lovely bit of green and a village hut/hall type thing. There was a bucket on a stand there which looked like it might have been part of the V. E. Day celebrations or possibly some Satanic rites. Maybe there is more going on in Horningsea than I might have imagined.

I romped around the funky little green area for a while and then spun off down the road a little. On Clayhithe Road there is a public footpath that points across the fields to the right. I've got lost on this footpath before, so thought I would give it another try to see what would happen this time. As soon as I got on to the field I was confronted with three choices.

The one to the right said absolutely no entry; there were nesting birds and I should not be stomping along there disturbing them. I thought that it was awfully late in the year for nesting birds and that they should damn well hatch or get off the nest, but I chose the path that seemed to loop around the hill and head for this huge electricity pylon (although I'm told by someone who used to work with mapping infrastructure that I shouldn't call them pylons – apparently their proper name is towers).

I encountered a field of food that I decided was probably corn and, joy of joys, there had been a path cut right through the middle of it. It's such a relief while running through fields to have the way so clearly marked; I always worry that I might be straying onto areas where I'm unwelcome.

I ran on through the fields and arrived at the pylon/tower thing. There was an abundance of signs here. Which way should I go?

Well, I'd just come from Horningsea, so probably not that one.

Fen Ditton was a possibility, but it would take me back towards home and I wasn't ready to turn around yet. Quy was a good possibility but wait, there was another option around the far side.

To Lode, it said, or if I wanted to be really adventurous I could go all the way to Wicken Fen. I decided to go to Lode and then consider which way to turn at that point.

I ran on down the path and eventually reached a road. There were a few houses here which I decided are probably Lode, and another sign.

It was very tempting to run down toward Bottisham and the river.

Hmmm – I took stock and realised that my legs were actually starting to hurt a little, so I should start to circle around back toward home. I shall leave Bottisham Lock for another day. I turned right into the picturesque village of Lode. It's a breathtakingly beautiful little village: lots of thatched cottages, modern bungalows, and some touches of Georgian splendour.

One of the joys of being out on a run with no pre-planned route is that I can take off in any direction I wish. I took advantage of this freedom in Lode, darting off down a number of little alleys and alluringly beautiful pathways. I found a village green and something called Fassage Hall, which sounds terribly old and grand but is actually a very modern-looking village hall. It looked a splendid purpose-built facility, although not quite what I expected. I startled a number of dog-walkers sauntering down the lanes. They all recovered quickly and wished me a cheery good morning as I wound around and about, taking in the delights of Lode.

There were so many things I would have liked to photograph but I was trying to tell myself not to bugger about quite so much and actually do a bit of running. I couldn't run past this building, though, without stopping to take a picture.

I've no idea what it is but it is a little bit special, I'm sure you'll agree.

I continued onwards until I encountered the National Trust property, Anglesey Abbey. It was closed but I was tempted into the grounds by a public footpath sign. Surely this won't take me too far out of my way, I thought, and I'll just loop around the grounds and back out onto the road a little bit further down. I ran across the car park and down through the trees. There were many pathways there, but I didn't see any signage so had no idea which way I was going or even whether I was still on the public footpath.

I passed a couple walking their dog and they waved and smiled as I ran by. There was a tiny river/stream here and I followed its track as it emerged from the trees and snaked away into what looked like an endless chain of fields stretching as far as the eye could see. I followed the path for some time, but it became more and more impassable as it continued onwards. My run quickly changed to a strange hopping, skipping and delicate sideways shuffle as I tried to avoid being nettled or scratched by brambles. I decided that this was probably no longer a path and turned back. I met the dog-walking couple down the trail a little and decided that maybe I should ask for some directions.

“You’ve probably figured out I’m lost,” I said as I ran back towards them.

“No, no,” they said. “We thought you’d just had enough and were coming back.”

I assured them that I was, in fact, quite lost and was trying to head towards Stow cum Quy and then to curve back towards Fen Ditton from there. They assured me that my route through the impassable brambles was the correct one, and that if I persevered then Stow cum Quy would be within my grasp. I turned back and fought my way through the undergrowth once more.

It went on and on and on, but eventually it became more like a path and I discovered something that actually looked like a dirt track that might lead to somewhere significant.

I stepped out onto the track and was confronted by another dog-walker. I hailed her and asked whether I was heading in the right direction for Stow cum Quy. She assured me that I was. She was tall, with brown hair swept back into a ponytail, and wearing dark glasses. She looked like a French film star hiding from her millions of fans in darkest Cambridgeshire. She moved like a dancer and when she raised her hand to point the way I had to fight the impulse to applaud her grace and beauty. I thanked her profusely and continued onwards.

Stow cum Quy was soon upon me and I turned right to head toward Newmarket Road. This is a lovely little footpath that somehow manages to duck and weave away from the crazy roundabout that will take the eager motorist onto the mega-highway that is the A14. The path leads you down onto Newmarket Road and on through the Park and Ride site to Fen Ditton. I then found the footpath that took me to the church and onto the village green.

It's while running through these places that I realise how fortunate I am to live where I do. In one run I had been through several villages – Horningsea, Lode, Stow cum Quy, Fen Ditton, and my own village of Milton – and all of them were just so breathtakingly beautiful. This is an absolutely splendid place to live.

I went through Fen Ditton but was really starting to suffer now. My legs were hurting and my drinking water was completely gone. However, there's a house in Fen Ditton where they fly several different flags and often put out a sign saying what those flags are. They also have a water fountain in their garden on the roadside, so I tried it out and found that beautiful clear cool water came from it that was just downright heavenly. Whoever is in that house, thank you, thank you, thank you. You are doing a wonderful thing providing water to the desperate and needy such as me.

I ran on through the village and then down to the river. I crossed over the River Cam at Baits Bite Lock and then back through Milton. I'd done 25 kilometres but was completely exhausted. Still, it gave me great confidence that I was on track to achieve the marathon distance: just another 17 kilometres to go.

However, it wasn't all going to be plain sailing.

So Many Injuries

My path to the London Marathon has had several strategically difficult injuries strewn across it.

The most common evils to visit have been tears (interesting that tears in muscles and eye-watering tears of pain and distress are the same word) in my calf muscles and hamstrings.

I'm still very much a novice as regards all this running stuff and so haven't yet figured out how to avoid these injuries. However, reading various blogs it looks like even experienced runners have their share of injuries. I am guessing that this is an area we know very little about and maybe in a hundred years or so we will have some sensible advice regarding how to care for your muscles and ligaments when running.

I got the opportunity to chat to a physiotherapist at the St Ives 10k. She told me a little about what happens to muscles when they tear and it sounded quite terrifying. Apparently the muscle rips apart and begins to bleed. This is where you see bruising on the leg. If it has gotten to that stage then it can take around three months to heal. THREE MONTHS! That's a long time to lay off running. A very long time to spend gazing out of the window, imagining how good it would feel to be out there roaming around.

The physiotherapist showed me various exercises with a foam roller (those roller things hurt but apparently they are quite good for you. Maybe it's like unpleasant-tasting medicine: the nastier it is, then the better it is for you. That's what my mother told me anyway). One of the strangest and most useful things that the physio mentioned was how to rehabilitate during the healing process. Apparently stretching is really important as otherwise the muscle can heal in a contracted position, all covered in scar tissue, and lock in a much tighter state than it should be. A most alarming thought, which spurred me on to a daily ritual of stretching exercises for calf muscles, hamstrings and quadriceps.

More Fundraising

There were so many things that I wanted to do but suddenly the marathon is all too close and we are fast running out of time. I keep up the pressure with social media and my blog posts. I cross-post everything to Facebook and Twitter so I am reminding people about the marathon and the fundraising.

Nearly all of the posts are tightly focussed on a run or something connected with my preparations for the upcoming marathon. I reckoned continually posting 'please donate' would soon sound like a mindless background buzz and could cause annoyance rather than inflame people with the desire to hand over lots of cash to save them rhinos and encourage Jim to run around London. I'll let you into a secret here. I didn't really need all that much encouragement to run the London Marathon. Even had you been so cruel as to turn your backs on those rhinos I would have laced up and gone out regardless. I am awfully grateful, though, that so many of you did donate.

I asked the chap looking after the local village website to post a little news story and he was good enough to do so. I was in the *Cambridge Evening News*. I appeared in all the run reports from the parkruns that I attended in the rhino suit. My story was written up in the Daily Briefing at my workplace (Cambridgeshire County Council) and I made sure that I mentioned the London Marathon at every gathering I attended. There was rarely a deluge of donations, but the continuous gentle nudging approach did serve to remind people about the fundraising. That meant that it was in their mind and had been reinforced several times when they were in a position to whip out the card, log onto the website, and donate their money through my Virgin Money Giving site.

One of our fundraising plans that was carried through was the bake sale. The reason this happened when so many other things didn't is because it was my wife, Carrie, organising this. She is fantastically determined and if she has decided that she will do something then it is almost certainly going to happen even if she has to part the waves of an ocean, move a couple of minor cities, and calm the rumblings of a volcano. She encountered some obstacles on the way to bake sale heaven but fortunately no volcanoes were harmed in the process.

For anyone wondering, she did chocolates (pouring melted chocolate into a rhino mould), biscuits (regular cookie-style biscuits cut to shape with a cookie cutter), and rhino cupcakes. The cupcakes were a standard chocolate chip cupcake recipe. Something like this:

200g Butter

200g Caster Sugar

3 Eggs

Vanilla Extract

200g Self Raising Flour

Half Teaspoon of Baking Powder

100g of Chocolate Chips

Preheat oven to around 180°C.

Beat together the butter, caster sugar, eggs and vanilla extract until the mixture is nice and smooth. Sieve the flour and baking powder into the mixture and combine.

Fold in the chocolate chips.

Spoon into bun cases and bake until golden.

Leave to cool on a rack.

Then get some white icing and grey icing and start cutting circles until you manage to get your rhino cupcakes to look a little like this:

She took the baked goods to her workplace and managed to raise £106.73.

Countdown To The Marathon

Training had been going quite well. I continued with my long runs and extended them even further. It was March now, with the London Marathon at the end of April; I had two 20 mile runs in the bag, and I was hoping to try out 22 or 23 miles the following week. Even my shorter runs seem to be getting a little faster.

Of course, this is all relative. I am a slow plodding kind of runner, so please don't picture a lithe leaping chap flowing through the landscape oozing grace, speed and style. I make progress by a strange kind of lurching momentum and sheer bloody-mindedness. It's not a pretty sight, but I do keep moving forward. And by sticking with the training, the speed and distance continued to increase. All was going well.

If this were fictional you would expect any good dramatist to crowbar a mishap into the tale at this point. However, this is real life and no crowbarring is required. Mishap just marches up to the door, smashes it down, waltzes in and makes itself at home. On 16th March, with only five-and-a-half weeks to go before the London Marathon, I find myself hobbling away from a Wednesday Up and Running social run with a torn hamstring. I am a very unhappy chap. This was shortly after a rapid increase in distance so, as with most of my running mishaps, entirely my own stupid fault.

I laid off running for a few days and then did a very gentle

11k at the weekend. It hurt a little but nowhere near as much as I expected. I felt a little hopeful but stayed away from running for another week. I then tried another parkrun (a tourist parkrun at South Manchester, when we were in the city for the UK national science fiction convention) and felt reasonable until around 4k, when the hamstring pain came back again and I looked a very sorry sight hobbling over the finish line.

Damn!

I went through another week of enforced rest but was all too aware that time was ticking away. We are into April now. This is the same month as the marathon and my training schedule is just blasted into tiny inconsequential pieces.

I tried out another fairly long run at the weekend and kept my stride really short in an attempt not to stretch the hamstring at all. It seemed to work. There was pain there but it felt like something that I could live with. My hopes were raised a little. On the following week those hopes were dashed once more as I began a parkrun and had to retire hurt after less than a kilometre.

We now have only two weeks to go and I am convinced that I won't be able to run the marathon. I am sure that any fitness that I had will be ebbing away and that this hamstring problem has crippled me so much that I shall break down before I reach the 10 kilometre mark. I decide to sit myself down and give me a good talking to.

Now Jim, you've read quite a lot of books about running and they all say that your running fitness is not easily lost. You have an injury and that's a bad thing, but you need to put it in perspective.

Firstly, it is quite likely that you will still get out there and run. You might not do all of it but you will be taking part in the London Marathon and that is a grand thing indeed.

Secondly, if you can rest between now and the marathon then maybe the hamstring will be OK. If that is the case then the fitness you have built up over the last year will carry you through to the end.

Thirdly, keep focussing on firstly (the opportunity just to even begin the London Marathon) and secondly (maybe the hamstring will heal in time). If you start trying to introduce a thirdly it will overheat your poor little brain and you'll forget those positives that you are trying to remember.

I managed to stay away from running for almost the entire last two weeks, but on the Friday before the marathon I couldn't help myself and went out for a very gentle 10k run. It felt OK. I did feel a little bit unfit. I did a little more huffing and puffing than I would expect to do – but I wasn't feeling any pain in the hamstring. Maybe it was going to be fine.

The Expo And The Night Before

It was finally here.

After all those months of training and excited anticipation, it was actually happening. I was going to run the London Marathon.

The day before the marathon, Carrie and I went along to the Expo at the ExCeL Centre to collect my race number. There was a huge hall full of queues and shops. We picked up my number at the start and then were funnelled, Ikea-style, around a route of gadgets, shirts, running accessories and invitations from around the world to join up to their dazzlingly exciting marathons.

So many places now have come to realise just how much money a big city marathon brings in to their local economy. Hotels, restaurants, transport systems all scoop up huge dollops of cash from the rampaging runners sweeping through their city. The runners stay a couple of days and then vanish as quickly as they came, leaving the various establishments sitting back and fingering excitedly through their recently accumulated wads of money.

The Expo is an exhausting experience. Carrie and I are weaving through the crowds, but every few minutes there seems to be some kind of mass migration and we are swept this way and that with little control over our own direction. I must admit that I am not entirely enjoying this experience. Crowds do tend to frighten me a little. Oh, what a good idea it is to run a big city marathon.

As we near the exit the space opens up a little, and we can almost begin to breathe again. There is an area for games where you can play to win extra donations for your charity. This sounds a most excellent idea, and Carrie and I both line up for the bowling alley. We fire the ball down the track and see the satisfying sight of a bunch of skittles all reclining happily after being well and truly bowled over. We claim our vouchers and take them to the harassed-looking laptop people, and they enter the details into their computer. Some day soon, they say, there will be an extra couple of five pound notes donated to Save The Rhino. Most excellent!

We then head out to the Docklands Light Railway, which is groaning under the strain of so many marathon runners trying to find their way to and from the ExCeL Centre. It's just about managing, but there is a rising note of hysteria in the voice of every announcer as they desperately try to herd us along and assure us that there will be trains some time in our future.

We are Greenwich-bound. Carrie booked us into the Mercure hotel in Greenwich so that getting to the start of the race would be a comfortable and relaxed experience.

On arriving at the hotel there is a titanic struggle through an irritating check-in procedure which seems to have been confounded by Carrie changing bank accounts and now having a different card to that with which she had booked the room. It's fair enough that they wish to check that you are the owner of the card, but it would have been nice if they had mentioned this in their booking emails so that old cards could be brought along to be checked.

We decided to eat in the hotel so that it will be a nice relaxed and easy night. They are doing a runner's special as the hotel is packed with London Marathon runners. We attended a seminar on nutrition at the Expo and they had advised that the evening meal should be before 8 pm so that it wouldn't be laying heavy upon us at 10 am the following day. They also advised that pasta would be good fuel so I, and many of the other runners there, had spaghetti bolognese. Unfortunately I probably ate quite a bit later than 8 pm as the service was massively slow. Maybe they weren't entirely geared up for this mighty glut of runners feasting upon pre-race carbohydrates.

We retired early and I was in quite a state of anxiety. I was experiencing all sorts of leg pain, mostly in my calves. I wondered if maybe I had been doing too much walking around that day and had strained something. This seemed unlikely as Carrie had no leg problems, so why should I be suffering so? Of course, it must have been psychosomatic, but it did feel very real indeed.

I laid out my kit all ready for the morning.

I had my buff. The buff is something I've only discovered recently. It's a bit of stretchy material you put over your head to wear as a kind of headscarf. Then when it gets warm you can wear it as a headband to keep the sweat from dripping into your eyes or as a scarf. It has many uses, but the one most commented upon by friends is that it makes it easier to spot me in a crowd.

There was the Save The Rhino T-shirt supplied by the Save The Rhino charity. I had this customised by local Cambridge T-shirt printing shop, Talking T's. They emblazoned the name Jim across my chest in letters as large as we could fit on the shirt.

There were the running shorts from Tesco and then my pride and joy, the Saucony Triumph ISO 2 running shoes. These are wonderful but had cost far more than I was accustomed to paying or could possibly afford myself (over £100). Fortunately I had prepared for this and asked several people at Christmas if they could contribute toward their cost (thanks especially to Carrie, my brother Tim, and Mum), and so I had truly amazing running shoes for the London Marathon.

My kit also included a small pouch known as a SPI belt. This is for Small Personal Items and is really useful for carrying things as I run. I also had an arm holder for my phone, which I strap around my bicep.

So there it is, all ready for me to wear tomorrow morning when I run the London Marathon.

Wait, what, tomorrow morning???!!!!

My London Marathon Run For Save The Rhino

Despite my anxieties that evening I still managed to get to sleep without too many problems and awoke early for breakfast. The nutritionist had recommended having breakfast three to four hours before the start of the marathon, so I tucked into the recommended egg on toast that they'd suggested would be just the thing. This was after a goodly number of us had decoded the mysteries of the diabolical toasting machine.

Egg and toast consumed, I was ready for my marathon. The leg pain seemed to have eased so I was hopeful that the many and various pains were all in my mind. Bring on this running thing. The time is now.

We left the hotel at about 8.30 am and wandered over to the park. We were soon joined by thousands of people all heading in the same direction. We reach the entrance to the runners' section, and this is where Carrie and I must part.

This is a peculiar moment. It's the point where I am no longer someone who may run the London Marathon at some time in the future. I go through this little arch, and I transform into someone who is doing the London Marathon right here and now. The terror begins to mount and I delay the moment that I must pass under the arch, which has now become massively symbolic. It is an entrance to another dimension which is a place of wonder and terror.

I think Carrie has seen my reticence and she seems quite happy for us to seek out a place to take yet another few last-minute photographs. Fortunately Carrie knows me well and doesn't ask too many questions about my odd behaviour. She nods and smiles as I burble away, trying to talk about anything other than the fact that I am about to run 26.2 miles. We take some more photos. I breathe deeply and go through the arch.

As one of the slower runners I was allocated red 9 pen, which is right at the back of everyone. The benefit of this was that I was with all the fancy dress runners, so the sights were absolutely amazing. I was fortunate enough to get an opportunity to chat with some of the Save The Rhino runners running in full rhino gear. I had run eight parkruns in the costume over Christmas, so we were able to share info about the difficulties of running in 10 kilogrammes of ridiculously hot rhino.

It was fortunate that today, at 10 degrees Celsius with a brisk wind, the weather would help to cool the rhino runners a little and so enable them to finish without heat exhaustion taking its toll. We also talked about the possibilities of the elites being able to achieve a really good time as the conditions were perfect for marathon running.

The weather did help as Eliud Kipchoge won with a course record of 2:03:05. He and Stanley Biwott battled for mile after mile, but at 25 miles he just stretched out and finished way out in front, in a course record and just eight seconds outside the world marathon record. Those times, so close to the magical two hours that may never be beaten, seem miraculous to me. The elite runners look so devastatingly beautiful, striding out as they cover the ground so easily and gracefully. My only regret is that we have so few British runners among the current crop of great marathon runners. The best this year was Callum Hawkins, at 2:10:52. I'll be interested to see how he does at the Olympic games in Rio. (He finished ninth there, running one minute longer for 2:11:52.)

Some time after the marathon we stayed with friends in Dunfermline. One of our hosts, Paul, who is himself an ultra-runner, asked me what I intended to achieve with my running. I have thought about this many times and struggled to find an answer. This time I think I was able to describe what I wanted to do rather better than anything I had previously articulated. I particularly love my long runs and delight in having developed enough strength and fitness that I can cover a significant number of miles to roam around and spend a considerable amount of time out in nature, just running around and seeing what is there.

I watch these Kenyan and Ethiopian athletes and adore the way they can stride out and eat up the miles. I want to de

velop more strength, power and stamina so that I can stretch out and churn through these miles in a similar way to these glorious athletes. I will never have the speed and power of Kipsang, Biwott or Kipchoge, but if I can just grab a faint glimmer of that power and roam around the villages of Cambridgeshire as a runner then I will have a feeling of being superhuman. I will have the feeling that my body is capable of extraordinary things and can go exploring while relying upon the strength that I have built myself through my own dedication and motivation.

Kipchoge won with a time of 2:03:05 but we got some good times from the British runners. After Callum Hawkins, Tsegai Tewelde was the second Brit at 2:12:23, and Derek Hawkins came in at 2:12:57.

However, all this elite running stuff was still to happen, and for the moment I was milling around with thousands of other people in Greenwich Park getting ready to run. First stop in the running enclosure was the baggage drop. This process was wonderfully efficient, with a line of trucks arranged by running number order and huge numbers of people waiting by the trucks ready to stow your bag with its runner number displayed. I had put some warm clothing into the bag as I knew that I always had trouble getting my body back up to temperature after a long run. My body dumps heat with alacrity during a long run, but once I have stopped I know that I soon become very cold indeed.

The running enclosure hosted the ever-present toilet queues. Whenever I've taken part in a race there are nearly always portable toilets and huge snaking queues inching slowly forward as we approach the start time. I didn't particularly need the toilet but thought that maybe I should go to see if I could stave off the need during the race. I looked at the queue and my heart sank.

I feel that a queue is such an astoundingly depressing thing. It kind of makes me feel trapped and unable to relax: I've held my place in the queue and must remain vigilant lest someone try to take the place in which I've invested so much time and effort. Of course I realise that is all a bit ridiculous. A queue could be quite a pleasant and relaxed experience. If you're in a queue you have something in common with everyone else there. You could use that commonality to strike up a conversation with anyone around you, even if it is something so banal as pointing out how slowly the queue is moving. From there you could continue on to all manner of discussions and really enjoy the company of the people around you. I know this is the right thing to do. Unfortunately when I'm in a queue I tend to close in on myself and just endure. I hope that eventually I can open up a little more to the people around me, relax and just enjoy being with folks.

This time I am fortunately saved from the queue when I see that there is a separate urinal enclosure for the men, and so I use that. It even has a hand-washing facility. Sheer luxury.

10 am approaches and Tim Peake, orbiting the Earth in the International Space Station, counts us down to the start. Tim is also running the marathon, chained to a treadmill out there in the space station. I am a little envious of him being able to run without his weight dragging him down. I am quite heavy at 85 kilogrammes, so would welcome not having to cope with the pull of

gravity. (I had been 90 kilogrammes, so have thankfully shed a significant amount of weight, but am still somewhat chunky.) One advantage I do have over Tim is that I will be running through one of the most beautiful and historic cities in the world, cheered on by thousands of people all willing me towards the finish line. That's got to beat running on a treadmill, even if it is somewhere as groovy as the International Space Station.

There is a radio commentary going on as we walk forwards towards the start line. The chap on the microphone is more or less saying anything that comes into his head. One of his comments is in adulation of all the beautiful women he can see on their way to the start: "Great to see so many beautiful women here today. There are also some ugly ones. Oh yes, you know who you are." Quite horrible, but I assume that he was trying to fill in time and keep talking, and some of his talk was just drivel.

There are several very large Wombles around. I wonder if we're going to pass Wimbledon and, if we do, will they stop to pick up litter?

We edge down to large iron park gates. There is a beautiful gatehouse there with a family living in it. A typical nuclear family of mummy, daddy, and two children are leaning out of the upstairs window waving at us. We all wave back merrily. At the next window, just set back a little, is an older woman. She waves too, although with a little more reticence. She seems slightly disengaged. Maybe she has arm wavey exhaustion from acknowledging this vast number of runners. I have to wonder whether the jolly little nuclear family in the next window even know that she is there.

After the house we turn the corner and can now see the start. There is another block of toilets, and many people run off in that direction for a last emergency visit before they cross the start timing mat. The excitement builds as we get closer to the large inflatable arch across the road signifying the start. The forward shuffling gets a little faster, and then suddenly everyone breaks out into a run. We are all packed in so tight that every movement seems to be in unison. The heads in front of me bob up and down as if they are in one giant wave motion. The clock at the start line reads 10:28. It has taken us 28 minutes just to reach the start, but now it has begun.

We all have just 26.2 miles to go.

Already I encounter people that have started walking. “We’re pacing ourselves,” they shout to all of us who have checked our stride and are running around them.

The weather still looks a little gloomy, but the temperature is fine. We head out towards Woolwich where the red, blue and green start routes all merge. Of course, everyone else has already passed this point, so any merging that there was to be done is now ancient history.

It is somewhere around here that I hear someone shouting “Jim!”. This is not so unusual; I have had my name put onto my Save The Rhino T-shirt to encourage folks to cheer me along. This, however, sounds a bit more insistent as if the person is trying to get my attention. I look up and it’s a face that I know from science fiction conventions. I wave back to Misha and feel warmed through and through. It felt good to see someone that I recognised on the streets of London.

I’m settling into my rhythm now. It can be quite difficult to keep up a steady pace in amongst so many people and so many distractions, but I had been warned what it would be like and had adjusted my expectations. I came to the London Marathon knowing that there would be absolutely no chance of running my own race at my own pace. It came as a very nice surprise on those few occasions where I did have a clear run. We turned back towards Greenwich, passed by on the opposite side of the park to that which I started on, and then we turned right to the Cutty Sark.

There was a fine swing band playing at the side of the road. I was feeling absolutely wonderful. I was so buoyed up by the crowds, the music, and the whole occasion that I felt almost superhuman. I was absolutely sure that I could run a thousand miles without breaking a sweat. I felt the urge to break off and dance to the swing band, but there was a little sensible voice in the dark recesses of my mind pulling me back. It warned me that I had a long way still to go and that all this excess energy I was experiencing would be better conserved for later. I gave a couple of little happy skips going past the band, but resisted the urge to dance.

Seconds later I am staring up at the massively impressive sight of the sailing ship, the Cutty Sark. I felt as if my breath had been snatched away. I was gasping in awe at the sight of the ship towering over me amid a backdrop of hundreds and hundreds of people, all yelling and waving from behind the barriers. There was music playing and a commentator talking to people in the audience and introducing the records.

It’s quite hard to describe just how much sound there was

in the area around the Cutty Sark. It feels almost as if someone has been roaming the Earth with their sound nets and then dumped it all in this small area for safekeeping. There is a feeling of helplessness as I wallow for a while in this giant cacophony. I stumble through this section in a daze and don't recover my composure until we cross Deptford Creek and are moving deeper into Deptford.

There's a long straight road now all the way to Surrey

Quays. I mentally do a check of my body and it's feeling fine. All those pains that I felt in my legs the previous evening seem to have completely disappeared.

There is a right turn at Surrey Quays and I get that tingling feeling as if there is some kind of presence. I peer over my left shoulder and sure enough, there is Silas with that intense stare of his. I am convinced that Silas has special powers. Standing together with Silas are Alan and Debs. All three of them are from ZZ9 Plural Z Alpha, *The Hitchhiker's Guide to the Galaxy* Appreciation Society. I turn around and run back to them. I give Debs a hug and shake hands with Silas and Alan; it's wonderful to see them all. I assure them that I am well and look forward to seeing them at the end on the Save The Rhino picnic blanket. I turn and wave and continue on with my marathon.

There is a little wiggle in the course after Surrey Quays and then the first set of showers. This is a collection of pipes at the side of the road that looks a bit like a spindly scaffold. You run up close to them and they blast out freezing cold water all over you. Most exhilarating, I thought, and so took every opportunity for a soaking whenever I saw one.

I pass a few more fancy dress superstars here. Most notable was probably the Jamaican Bobsleigh Team and a group of firefighters – complete with their own fire engine, which they carried with them. I didn't look too closely but I suspect it wasn't a real fire engine.

The spectators weren't to be outdone and they also provided considerable entertainment. One person carried a large, old-fashioned car horn with a sign offering "Free Honks". Others had signs offering free hugs, and one hopeful young lad had a sign that offered free kisses.

I think my favourite spectator strangeness was a very earnest-looking chap reading from a gospel and putting his heart and soul into it as he preached at the passing runners. We ran by and I heard one runner proclaim, "Did I just see...?" and someone else assured him that he had. Most bizarre.

There were many more bizarre sights along the route, including Jesus running with a wooden cross on his back. Apparently this was a chap called Makoto Takeuchi from a Japanese rock band called The Chambers Flag. He even ran without shoes, as he said that Jesus wouldn't have shoes so why should he.

We took a long looping run around Rotherhithe, and then followed the river for a while before turning to cross it at Tower Bridge. This is one of the iconic scenes from the London Marathon. Running up to the massive tower structure was awe-inspiring, exciting and exhilarating all at the same time. Runners all around me were stopping to take photos and maybe I should have too, but I was in some strange kind of floating trance looking at the tower and soaking up the atmosphere that surrounded me.

The noise level increased dramatically on the bridge. It was packed with madly exuberant charity team supporters. There were so many banners that I wondered if it was somewhere you could only get a place if you're connected with one of the major London Marathon charities. Do you perhaps have to pay for a spot on the bridge? Thinking about this, it seems unlikely that there is a fee to be there. It's probably just that all these charity supporters get there really early to bag a spot at one of the most photographed places in the London Marathon; it's an ideal spot to get your charity placards in photos and on television. I looked for Save The Rhino, but there was no sign of them. A great shame, but competition must be extremely fierce and Save The Rhino are tiny compared to some of the other charities involved.

The bridge goes uphill to the centre and then slopes pleasantly downhill on the other side. We are just approaching halfway and I am feeling deliriously happy. I have what probably looks like a ridiculous grin plastered permanently across my face. My legs are hurting, but it doesn't feel like anything that will cause me a problem. My breathing is easy and I'm feeling relaxed and in excellent spirits. All is good.

We turn right after the bridge, back toward the dock areas where we see runners on the other side of the road heading towards central London. They are moving fast and I envy the ease with which they cover the ground. I wonder for a moment whether anyone is ever tempted to jump over the central barrier to skip a few miles. I reckon it unlikely, partly because it would seem to negate the point of attempting to run the marathon – but, more prosaically, there are so many witnesses with cameras that such a move would very quickly make you a hate figure on Youtube. (Apparently there was a cheat who must have done something like this, the sister of a chap called James Argent who is in a TV programme, *The Only Way Is Essex*. She is Natasha Argent and claims that she had a panic attack and got confused. Natasha has now handed back her finisher's medal and is banned from any future events held by London Marathon Events.)

As we are running toward Canary Wharf, I glance around at my fellow runners. There seems to be a lot of social media stuff happening. There's a woman with a selfie stick posing dramatically for her camera phone. She's wearing makeup and looks very composed and glamorous as she flicks her hair back, pouting for the camera. A man also has his phone on a selfie stick and is giving race commentary as he runs. I hear him say, "Many of you may not have run a marathon before," as I run by, and wonder if he's broadcasting live or recording for a podcast.

I did consider creating a podcast myself, but then figured that for my first marathon I needed to concentrate on just running, if I was going to finish it. I also don't think I would want to spend the whole marathon carrying a phone on a selfie stick. I reckon I would be more likely to use a head-mounted video camera and maybe a separate audio device that had a fixed microphone, either as part of a headset or attached to my shirt. That would mean very little footage where I am in shot, but that may possibly be a factor in favour of the head camera.

Canary Wharf is ahead of us and then a run around the Isle of Dogs. Carrie should be waiting there and she said that she would try to get hold of a bag of peanuts for me. We have a theory that the salt may come in useful. I tend to lose quite a lot of salt when I run. I have heard people say that elite runners lick their own skin to replenish their salt, but I can't say that I have ever seen that happen.

Carrie has been reading up on all the spectator info and taken on board all the dire warnings about how difficult it is going to be to get around London with so many roads closed and the vast crowds of people milling around. It probably all has something to do with this marathon thing taking place here.

Her campaign began by seeing me off at the start area in Greenwich and then she was going to go through the tunnel, under the river, to the Isle of Dogs. Apparently it was harder to cross the marathon route than she expected and she did, quite by chance, encounter me running in Greenwich before she went to the tunnel. I didn't see her, though.

But at the Isle of Dogs she yelled out at me and waved a 'Don't Panic!' towel in my direction. That and the fact that she had warned me that she would be there meant there was no chance that I would miss her. We hugged and kissed, and she bestowed some dry roasted peanuts upon me.

Silas was there with her and gave me the good news that

the other folks from the *Hitchhiker's Guide to the Galaxy* Appreciation Society were waiting just a few yards further on. Sure enough, there they were, with another 'Don't Panic!' towel. I greeted them warmly and posed for photographs with the towel. I was still feeling quite good, although the large muscle in the front of my legs was really hurting. It felt like someone had shoved an iron bar under my skin and it was busily bashing up against all sorts of other more fragile bones and muscles in its vicinity. However, I still felt strong and surged on.

I had been wondering about a possible toilet stop for some time. Aware of the London Marathon's strongly worded advice that we shouldn't pee in people's gardens, I was looking for something slightly less antisocial. I did eventually find something, but it was still quite public. The lines at all of the portaloos were huge but I noticed, when we were under one of the bridges, that there was also a large round plastic thing with holes in it next to the portaloos. I nipped over and peed into one of the holes. Several of the blokes spotted me doing this and immediately left the portaloo queues.

"I saw these," said one of them, "but didn't realise they were toilets."

I was only about 70 per cent sure myself, but I peed in them anyway. The women queueing at the portaloos jeered at us. I think the phrase “lucky bastards” was uttered by one of our well wishers.

We emerged into the sunlight and I reckoned we were now pointing back in the direction of London. This should have been lifting my spirits, but I was now starting to feel quite unhappy. My pace had dropped and the distance markers seem to have become spaced further apart. I passed the 20 mile marker and tried cheering myself up. Only a 10k (or so) to go. All your training runs are at least 10k. This should be easy. It’s not really helping.

I look in vain for the 21 mile marker but it doesn’t seem to arrive. I am in a world of pain now and seem to have been running forever since that 20 mile sign. My mind could focus on nothing else. Where was that sign? Why didn’t I seem to be making any progress? I couldn’t be lost. It is quite impossible to lose your way on the London Marathon, so I must just have slowed down to a crawl. I slogged on, starting to feel really miserable, and even the joyful cries of all the happy spectators had faded to become just a background noise.

Then in the distance I saw a sign. I picked up my pace a little and craned my neck eagerly to see it as I got closer. I got a wonderful surprise when I saw that it was the 22 mile marker. Somehow I had managed to miss the one telling me that I had reached 21 miles. My mood swung way back and the big silly grin returned to keep me company. I was still in vast amounts of pain, but the change in mindset made it all so much more bearable.

Along the route there had been people handing out sweets and fruit, but I had resisted thus far apart from an orange segment near Tower Bridge which looked too deliciously tempting for me to refuse. Most marathon advice warns against eating anything that you haven't trained with. I had experienced much difficulty during my early long runs trying to figure out how to get the right amount and the right sort of nutrition into my body to keep it going. Some things laid too heavy, others made me feel sick and some just had no useful effect whatsoever. I had eventually arrived at a combination of ordinary water and Clif Shot Bloks. These are a solid gel-type thing and they seem to work for me.

During the race, though, it was very tempting to take some of the many goodies being offered to us by the crowds. Many parents had taken their children to watch the marathon and, to help keep them engaged in what was happening, had given them boxes and boxes of sweets to offer to the runners; I suspect that a goodly amount was eaten by the children, too.

I eventually did start taking sweets, as the look on the children's faces when you took Haribo or Jelly Babies from them was absolutely priceless. It really made them feel part of the London Marathon experience and their delight was almost palpable. It often became quite competitive, as children jostled with each other to make sure the runners took sweets from them rather than their siblings. I saw some particularly vicious tactics, all too often from the most angelic-looking children, that involved tripping, blocking and distraction.

There was another thing being offered at the side of the road that looked just downright strange. I encountered people wearing latex gloves that seemed to have something sticky all over them. It took me quite some time to figure out that this was probably Vaseline or something similar. It seems that the idea is that you high five these folks and come away with a hand soaked in goo. You then rub it wherever you might be sore. I am quite fortunate in that so far I have never had to use lubricant. I have only ever once had sore nipples and that was during a really torrential downpour, yet even then I only suffered mild discomfort.

I pushed on and passed a woman also wearing a Save The Rhino T-shirt. I smiled and offered her a cheery acknowledgement as a fellow Rhino runner. She returned me a look that could have curdled milk at 50 paces. I figured that she was probably in a bad place at that moment, so I hurriedly moved on.

The 22 mile happy boost moment is now a distant memory. Those quadricep muscles have stepped up the pain level several more notches. The soles of my feet feel as if they have been battered to a soft pulpy goo. I am convinced they must be all mashed up and damaged, but don't dare stop to look. If I remove my shoes then I'm sure they won't go back onto my feet again.

I've suffered during many of my runs but it's often worse during a race. I've racked my brains many times trying to figure out why this might be. My first thought was that I was trying that much harder. That would seem to make sense, but I'm not sure that I do try so much harder. Being very much a back of the pack runner, I know that making the extra effort to finish five seconds earlier is probably not going to make much difference to my overall placing. In a 38,000 person race it might mean that I come in at 33,210 instead of 33,213. Not even I, as centre stage leading actor in my own personal drama, would bother to raise even one eyebrow at such an improvement (although as an aside, I wish I could raise just one eyebrow at a time).

My second thought seemed to make more sense. At about two-thirds of the way through a race I start thinking about the end. I am counting down how much further I have to go and how long it is going to take me to get there. To start with, this seems to help a bit and the mathematics required distracts me from the fatigue in my legs. Then, I think, my brain takes this information and starts to feed back its conclusions. These conclusions are mostly that I am never going to make it to the end. The message is that I should slow down or walk or just sit down for a bit. Go on, whispers the tricksy brain. You know it makes sense. Just a few minutes' rest here and you'll be able to continue later.

This battle against the all-too-reasonable tricksy brain suggestions feels quite draining, and it is something that is rarely there in training runs. I don't usually plan how far I am going to run when I'm just clocking up a few miles on a Sunday morning. I go out, wander about for a while looking for interesting trails, and then come home again. It's exhausting, but I don't usually count down the miles and I very rarely have my brain telling me that I'm too tired to continue.

Obviously this is all conjecture but it feels like there is a link, so I probably need to try to distract myself from thinking how far there is to go if I am going to outwit my own tricksy brain. Today, though, in this London Marathon I am counting down and definitely feel that I'll never be able to keep going all the way to the end.

I am just about to pass under the end of Blackfriars Bridge when my phone begins to buzz. It's Carrie and she tells me that she and the ZZ9ers are waiting for me on the Embankment, somewhere around mile 25. I try to acknowledge what she was saying with some degree of coherence, but I probably wasn't too successful.

Talking to Carrie later, she tells me that this was quite a worrying phone call. I sounded absolutely terrible but she couldn't imagine any way that she could help so didn't comment on it at the time. This was probably for the best, as I'm not sure that it would have been useful for me if she had told me how appalling I sounded.

Into the dark we went, under the end of the bridge and

then up the hill into the sunlight once again. We were on the Embankment now and I was trying to talk myself around. I have read many books about marathon- and ultra-runners in which they often talk about repeating some kind of mantra to help them to push on when the pain threatens to overwhelm them. Apparently Paula Radcliffe chanted, “I love you Isla” (Isla being her baby daughter), in the New York Marathon to beat Geta Wami. Previously I couldn’t see myself doing this chanting stuff. How could repeating some string of words help to overcome physical distress?

Now, as I ran along the Embankment and waves of pain were washing over me, I was trying to think myself through it all. I knew that I hurt and had to accept that. I also felt it unlikely that the pain would get any worse. If I were to get to the end, all I had to do was keep putting one foot in front of the other. This thought sort of stuck in my mind and kept coming back in slightly different forms. One foot in front of the other, one foot at a time, keep moving one step at a time. All I had to do was to keep moving and eventually I would reach the end. It was all quite simplistic thinking but I was so exhausted I couldn’t string any kind of coherent thought together, and so I lapsed into a chant, repeating the same words over and over.

One foot in front of the other.

One foot in front of the other.

One foot in front of the other.

One foot in front of the other.

One foot in front of the other.

One foot in front of the other.

The pain and exhaustion was still there but my chanting drone somehow gave it all an air of unreality and maybe, just maybe, slightly took the edge off it.

The Embankment seemed to go on forever but eventually I saw the 25 mile marker. I was really suffering now and not taking too much notice of my surroundings. I was still repeating my mantra and moving forwards, but living in the midst of so much pain and suffering that my thinking and perception had reduced to a very basic level indeed.

I suddenly heard a huge amount of hysterical shouting over my shoulder. I turned to look and there were two young girls, an older man and two folk who were probably in their sixties. The girls were shouting loudest and they were all purple-faced, screaming, shouting, jumping and waving. "MUM! MUM!" they yelled. Then, huffing and puffing along the road came a woman, staring at the ground, shuffling along, obviously in some distress. She looked up and saw the two young girls screaming at her. A smile broke across her face as she staggered across and embraced them in a desperate hug.

I thought of these girls waiting for their mother and the sheer joy and elation they felt when they saw her. The huge outpouring of emotion felt so raw and so real. Before this day she had been just Mum to them, but now she was a hero who could run the kind of distance that other folk could only imagine doing in a car. Mum was now a super-being who had run the London Marathon. She was no longer just Mum to these girls. She was MY MUM who ran the London Marathon.

I envied this family their joy and rejoiced in it. It was a wonderful thing to witness and brought me to tears. Of course, at this stage of the race I was more than a little susceptible to a few tears.

A few yards further on, my own delightful supporters group of Carrie, Silas and Alan were all waiting for me and cheering madly. Yet again they managed to lift my mood, and I looked up to see the Houses of Parliament and the clock tower directly in front of me. I couldn't coax any more speed out of my legs, but the pain seemed to recede a little and I knew that there was no way that I wasn't going to finish. I was near enough now that I could crawl to the end if I had to.

I turned right along Great George Street and Birdcage Walk, and the sound volume suddenly increased massively. Waves of noise and outpourings of emotion washed over all of we runners staggering along that last mile. Both sides of the road were lined with thousands of people urging us on. I was laughing and crying at the same time, trying to cope with a crazy mixture of feelings.

Then there was the final turn on Spur Road up the Mall, and yet again more waves of sound rolled over us as we staggered onwards.

The last few hundred yards were both too long and too short. I was savouring the joy of having reached the finish but wondering why it was taking so long to cover such a short distance. I kept turning my legs over, but I could barely feel anything below the waist now. My legs were numb and my perceptions were reduced to monosyllabic acceptance of just having arrived at a point where all this pain would soon be over.

I crossed the line and staggered onwards. Someone hung a medal over me and I felt I was sagging under the weight of it. My legs still felt numb, but once I stopped they began sending back messages of gratitude to me for discontinuing the torture.

Onwards we went and picked up plastic bags with T-shirts and various promotional items and then onto the lines of trucks with our drop bags. I quickly found mine and then walked very slowly to the side of the road. I staggered over to some stands where folks were taking our pictures and then went to lean on one of the fence posts. I intended to do a few stretches on these posts, and then found myself staggering unsteadily while seeing black spots before my eyes. I wobbled a little and my head felt incredibly hot. What to do next? I thought that I should sit down before I fell, but then there was the worry that I might not be able to get back up again.

Glancing around, I saw a St John's Ambulance tent only a few yards away. I lurched toward it trying to ask for assistance but not really managing any proper words. It will have looked almost exactly like the march of a particularly slow-moving zombie. Fortunately the chap at the tent was made of stern stuff, so not even my march of the undead could faze him. He grabbed hold of my arm and guided me to a chair. He asked me what the problem was and I managed to convey that I felt as if I was going to faint. He handed me a funnel for puke and then some water. I attempted to take a drink. My head began to cool, but then I started to worry that the problem may have shifted. I sat there thinking that I desperately needed to go to the toilet but just couldn't move. I feared that the consequences might be disastrous and extremely embarrassing, but there was nothing I could do.

Then something happened that took my mind off any potential toilet problems as I got a really nasty calf cramp. Suddenly I am screaming and a chap with an armband saying doctor is knelt at my feet, grabbing my foot.

"Is it calf cramp?" he asks. I nod vigorously.

He bends my foot up and asks me to point my toes toward my chin. This stretches out the muscles in the calf and the pain subsides. He asked me what I had been eating and drinking and I said mostly just water and a few Shot Bloks.

"Here, drink this," he says. He offers me a Lucozade isotonic drink that had a packet of some kind of energy powder dumped into it. "It'll taste foul," he says, "but it should help to stop any more cramps." He's right, it does taste foul but I don't get any more cramps so maybe it was just what I needed.

Eventually the nausea and the desperate need to visit the toilet fades and I am just left feeling very cold indeed. Someone wraps me in a blanket and then some foil to try to keep me warm. I stay there for quite some time, shivering away, but eventually reckon I should move on and try to find Carrie. I express my gratitude and stagger out of the tent.

At the end of the finishers' funnel is a group of people with Save The Rhino banners. I tell them that I'm a Rhino runner and someone leads me away to their picnic blanket. They photograph me and try to shovel food inside my rather confused body. I'm busily shivering, so not sure I can cope with something as complicated as eating and being cold at the same time. Silas, Alan and Carrie are all there and are soon admiring my huge chunk of medal. It is a very significant-looking thing indeed and becomes the star of many photographs.

I am still struggling to get warm, so soon suggest that we move off somewhere to get a hot cup of coffee. London is at our feet, so we reckon there should be a coffee shop or two about the place. We struggle slightly, due to it being Sunday and there being rather a lot of people about, but very soon I am sipping coffee and heat is beginning to return to my body. I start to feel almost human again and begin to tell stories from my run. Unfortunately I find that I am also beginning to droop a little and there is a distinct danger that I shall fall asleep.

We say goodbye to the ZZ9ers. Carrie and I head for the river bus and are soon making our way back to Greenwich and the hotel.

In the next few days there was a considerable amount of pain, particularly in my quads. Going down stairs was almost impossible unless I turned around and went backwards. However, by the following Saturday I was able to run a parkrun and then the Fen Drayton 10k only 7 days after the marathon.

Although it didn’t seem possible at first my body does seem to be recovering. This is fortunate as I have another marathon coming up in only a month. The general advice seems to be that it takes about a week per mile to recover after such a long run. I've heard this advice so I know another marathon is a silly idea, but I still intend to do it. I had entered the Edinburgh Marathon as they had an offer that you could back out if you got a London Marathon place. When I did manage to get a London place, I decided to see if I could manage Edinburgh too.

I have also achieved my target of raising £2,500 for Save The Rhino International. A great big thank you to all of you folks who donated, and thank you to everyone who offered me encouragement on my journey to and through the London Marathon. It was a most amazing, wonderful and astounding experience. It took me five and a quarter hours to complete, so I missed my target of getting under 5 hours but somehow it just didn't seem to matter.

Watching The Marathon (How To Get Around London On Marathon Day)

There are a lot of people on the streets of London on marathon day. The BBC estimated something like 750,000 people came out to watch the marathon, which is brilliant for the runners, but if you are trying to navigate around London to support your runner then there are going to be some challenging times ahead.

My wife, Carrie, researched the options as much she could before race day, but many of the websites just warned about how difficult it was going to be and related horror stories from previous years of people getting delayed at tube stations and missing their runner completely. The Virgin Money marathon website itself was one of the best sources of information. There were plenty of maps breaking the course up into chunks so you could get some idea of good places to aim for.

Carrie decided to keep it as simple as possible. She would walk along to the start and see me off. This was reasonably easy as we'd stayed overnight in a hotel quite close to the park. She would then walk through the foot tunnel at the Cutty Sark to get to the Isle of Dogs somewhere around mile 16. This had looked as if it was going to be one of the quieter spots, so she reckoned she could get quite close to the runners and I should be able to spot her. This place also had the benefit of it being possible to get there without using public transport. Most of the spectator advice online warned that it would be nothing short of Tubemageddon on the London

Underground that day.

After the Isle of Dogs she would then hop onto a riverboat to meet me at the Save The Rhino picnic blanket at the end. It must have been a good plan, as it worked and she managed to squeeze in two extra sightings of me running the marathon.

On the day, Carrie and I walked over to Greenwich Park and we parted company at the runner's compound. She then managed to find her way around so that she could see me lined up at the start through the railings. I didn't see her at first and some confusion ensued when the chap next to me thought she was waving at him. We lost contact soon after that as there was no easy access for her to get through to the start from where she was, but she was content that she'd seen me on my way.

The next part of the plan was to get to the foot tunnel near the Cutty Sark. Here Carrie encountered a spoke in the wheel or fly in the ointment or potential plan scupperer: she could find no places to cross the course. It was beginning to look like the marathon had taken over so much of Greenwich that you were consigned to one side of the course or the other for the whole day.

She then also realised that there was a small ray of sunshine forcing its way through her clouds of trapped-on-the-wrong-side despair. She was on Greek Road, just after the Cutty Sark, and I must shortly pass by. I did pass by her and she got to see me running – but unfortunately I didn't manage to see her amongst the massed ranks of loud screaming folk that came to see us there.

Eventually Carrie found a spot without crash barriers and summoned up the courage to dart across the course in a space between the runners, to a chorus of tutting from the crowd. Carrie hung her head and scuttled away to the foot tunnel under the river. There were huge queues here for the lift, so she used the stairs and found it to be not as crowded as she'd feared. The tunnel had been made one way for this period of time as it was a popular route for people spectating the marathon.

She emerged from the tunnel to find some enterprising souls stationed there selling sandwiches and cakes. She bought a smoked salmon and cream cheese bagel, which was a very welcome smackerel indeed. One of the things that wasn't welcome was the lack of public toilets around. There were portaloos, but Carrie had witnessed far too hellish and evil portaloos in her lifetime to risk getting anywhere near one now. The public toilets all seemed to have been closed for the duration. She did manage to find a toilet in a pub on Westferry Road near mile 16, and then unsuccessfully tried to buy a drink. Queuing for beer in any pub near the London Marathon course on marathon day is a major commitment in time.

Carrie then searched for a quiet spot to wait for me to come by, but it seemed that even here on the Isle of Dogs there were no quiet spots. She did manage to find some railings to lean on and squeezed in there waiting for me to come by. She was soon joined by Silas who was part of the ZZ9 contingent that had come out to support me. (ZZ9 had contributed £250 towards my fundraising total. The individual members had also contributed a similar amount.) Two more ZZ9ers (Debs and Alan) had stationed themselves a little further down the road to cheer me on and give me that extra little boost needed to escape the Isle of Dogs.

Carrie phoned me and this time I found her quite easily. I stopped at her spot by the railings to collect a bag of nuts and some much needed hugs. Likewise I also found Debs and Alan who didn't have any nuts for me but hugs were plentifully available. Debs then went home and the rest of them embarked on the last leg of their journey via the river bus. This is a lovely way to get around London. It's a little more expensive than the Underground but much nicer and, on race day, considerably less crowded.

They went down to the Embankment on the boat and then spotted that there were actually quite a few gaps next to the barrier there. They stopped there, hoping to see me one more time before I got to the finish. Carrie phoned me as I was passing mile 24 and was rather shocked at the distant and despairing voice she heard at the other end of the call. She thought of pointing out how terrible I sounded and then thought that this may not be the best encouragement to get me through my final two miles.

I spotted them again at mile 25 and then they had the difficult task of crossing the course again to get to the finish area. Fortunately local knowledge came in useful here and they were able to use Westminster tube station to get under the road and across the course. It was a place of pandemonium and a high density of humans, but they struggled through and managed to find a group of Save The Rhino volunteers near the finish who directed them to the picnic blanket.

There they waited and waited, chatting to the friendly Save The Rhino photographer chappie and wondering where I had got to.

When I arrived, Carrie says she didn't recognise me at first. I was all shrouded in blankets and looked like I was a very ill person who had been sleeping rough for quite some time. We were reunited and eventually I made enough of a recovery to seem almost recognisable again.

So, Carrie's race day plan had worked and she had even managed to squeeze in an extra couple of sightings of me on the course.

I offer here a few of Carrie's tips for London marathon day spectating.

1. *If you possibly can, stay somewhere close to the start on the night before.*
2. *Wear sensible shoes: there will be much walking.*
3. *Use the river bus to get around London.*
4. *There will be a shortage of toilets, so if you get the opportunity to use one then take it.*
5. *Don't expect to easily get a drink in any pubs*

near the course.

6. *Plan in advance where you intend to see your runners.*
7. *Track your runners using the app or the website.*
8. *Take an emergency charger for your phone. You will drain the battery taking photos and using the maps feature.*
9. *The foot tunnel by the Cutty Sark is a splendid thing indeed and highly recommended to get to places further along the course after you leave Greenwich.*

Another Marathon Because I Don't Want to Be A Chap Who Has Only Run One Marathon

I am running alongside the sea, heading out of Edinburgh, and everything seems to be going well. There is some pain in my knee but it has dissolved into a background ache rather than the grinding hurt I had felt before. I am enjoying the course and I feel pretty good. Despite all my fears it seemed that this, my second marathon, was going to go much smoother than I expected.

So why was I so fearful about this run?

Well, it had all begun a few weeks ago. I had run the London Marathon four weeks previously and, even though I had emerged aching and hurting, I had suffered no injury. I rested for a week afterwards and then settled back into my usual running routine. All the next week was fine until Friday when I popped out for a nice gentle 10k around the park and along the path next to the busway.

Near the end of this run I felt a bit of a twinge in my knee. Hmmm, slightly unsettling, thinks I, but I'm sure that it's nothing to worry about. A couple of hours later I was finding it quite painful to walk. Every time I bent my knee, the back of the kneecap felt as if it was scraping backwards and forwards over jagged glass. I went to parkrun the following day and only managed the first kilometre before I limped sadly from the course. With the Edinburgh Marathon only two weeks away, drastic action was called for. I rang around and booked an appointment with a physiotherapist.

The physiotherapist that I chose was from Vinery Studios in Cambridge. Darryl from the local running shop, Up and Running, told me that they had been doing some work with Vinery Studios so I thought I would give it a go. I booked an hour session with Michelle for Tuesday, very much hoping that she would be able to help.

Michelle looked at my leg, asked me some questions and did a bit of prodding. She then got me to lay down and do various leg raises in different positions.

“I’m going to push down on your leg and I want you to resist as hard as you can.”

I resisted and the leg was pushed down as easily as you might slide a glass along a polished table. She readjusted me and instructed me to resist again. The sliding glass on polished table thing repeated itself all too easily. Michelle made her diagnosis.

My quads, it seems, are reasonably strong. Apparently this is often the case with runners. It’s one of the muscles that we very much rely upon. Michelle tells me the strong muscle interacting with the weak muscles will have pulled the knee out of alignment. This causes it to scrape against things that it shouldn’t be scraping against. She gave me a bunch of exercises to do and I went home and set to, in the hope that I could whip these muscles into shape before the Edinburgh Marathon.

I tried out out my knee the following weekend and, although it was fairly painful, it didn't feel too bad. I ran 16k and my confidence soared. Running the Edinburgh Marathon now looked like something that I might be able to do. I saw the physio again the following Tuesday and she seemed pleased with my progress. I could do all those fancy clever things like walking up and down stairs.

"Do you think I might be able to run the Edinburgh Marathon?" I asked hopefully. Michelle thought it might be possible but advised me to stop if it began to hurt.

I floated away in a sea of happy complacency until I came to do a gentle run two days before the marathon. The pain was back and it continued after I had stopped running, inflicting all sorts of hideous discomfort upon me. I checked the website to see whether it would be possible to get a refund or a deferral if I pulled out of the Edinburgh Marathon, but it assured me that they didn't hold truck with any of that sort of thing. I resolved to run but knew that having to quit during the race was a distinct possibility.

So I'm running along and thinking that maybe things are going to be OK. The course is nice, although it maybe seems a little disingenuous calling it the Edinburgh Marathon when so little of it is in Edinburgh. Maybe something such as East Lothian Marathon or Musselburgh Marathon might be more appropriate, or possibly they could get really cocky and call it the Scottish Marathon. This latter suggestion might possibly upset all those other people who run marathon events in Scotland.

We run around a few streets in Edinburgh and then head out to the coast. There is mile after mile of sea and sand on our left hand side and a lovely cooling breeze coming off the sea. Everyone is now settling down to their regular pace after the hustle and bustle of the first seven or eight kilometres.

A chap called Steve runs alongside me and begins to chat. He's from Woking and is telling me how much marathons terrify him. He sounds as if he is faster and more experienced than I at this thing, but the marathon still frightens him every time. We compare training and talk about all those runner-type things such as intervals, long runs, hydration etc. – all those topics that we can put non-runners to sleep with at dinner parties. Steve is also worried about injury problems and feels that he hasn't had the training that he would like to have had. We compare trials and tribulations, but also look to chat about the good things such as the scenery and that astoundingly welcome sea breeze.

Musselburgh eventually hoves into view and is a welcome sight. Even though we are only a third of the way through, we know that next time we come into Musselburgh the race will be done. We make progress.

I am enjoying the interaction with the spectators although am acutely aware of the vast difference between this event and the London Marathon. In London the levels of craziness just seem to go higher and higher. People are screaming and shouting and encouraging each other to become massively excited about the whole experience. The crowds infect the runners with their excitement and the runners respond, so encouraging the crowds even more.

In Edinburgh there is support but it is more at the level I am accustomed to in the smaller races that I have taken part in around Cambridge. There are some people shouting out, especially as I am wearing my London Marathon Save The Rhino T-shirt with my name emblazoned across the front. I make sure that I acknowledge every shout; I feel obliged to do so but don't feel that this is a bad thing. Obligations can often feel like a burden, but this one feels an absolute joy.

Looking across the road we see the leaders start to come through. The winner was a chap called Kiprono. I hadn't heard of him before this.

I was imagining myself coming back this way and really looking forward to it. It was a gentle downhill and the breeze would be behind me, urging me onwards.

At around 15 miles Steve asked me for his Lucozade bottle. I dug around in his backpack and handed it to him. My leg was hurting so I cadged some ibuprofen gel from him. His tendons were hurting and he asked me to rub some gel on his knee also.

Steve ran on; I stepped out to try to catch up and found the knee pain had increased dramatically. I gritted my teeth and tried to carry on and then suddenly discovered that I could no longer put any weight on my left leg without it buckling from the pain. I staggered over to the side of the road and found a tree to prop myself up against with one leg held in the air. A marshal came to help, asked if I needed medical assistance and I said yes.

While we were waiting I heard various exchanges on his radio. Not everyone was as willing to stop and receive assistance. Someone else apparently was weaving all over the road in considerable distress, bumping into other runners. Marshals had asked him to stop but he didn't seem to hear them and carried on. Someone was shouting over the radio, "Stand in front of him, it's the only way to stop them when they're like this."

I had no such problems stopping myself running. Putting any weight at all on that leg sent huge rolling waves of agony flashing out sharply from my knee. I wasn't keen on the notion of letting that foot touch the ground any time soon.

The doctor appeared a few minutes later and offered me several tablets. I swallowed them down and then he asked me what I was going to do. I was a bit nonplussed by the question as I didn't feel that I had much in the way of options. I decided that telling him that I was just going to stand here on one leg and whimper probably wasn't an answer that anyone wanted to hear. Instead I suggested that maybe I would try to find my wife, who had said that she would try and connect up with me at mile 16. I reckoned that I was past mile 15 but wasn't entirely sure. The doctor and the marshal didn't know where we were other than in their sector thirteen.

I reckoned that I needed to get moving and put my left foot down to try walking. I howled in pain and stopped again. I called Carrie and told her the news. She said that she was in a taxi trying to find the course and asked where I was. I couldn't really give her any specific information. I tried to walk again and found that if I kept the knee very straight indeed it could bear a little weight. I limped forward. People were asking me all the time whether they could help, but there wasn't much that anyone could do. What I needed was transport to the end to collect my baggage, but no one was in a position to offer me that. Some kind people did give me a bottle of orange juice, though, and that was very welcome indeed.

The doctor caught me up again and pointed across the other side of the road. There was a footpath going up to a village. He reckoned that might be a good way to connect up with my wife. I concurred and attempted to cross the road. There was a constant stream of runners but eventually I saw a gap and, with the speed of a snail attempting to slide across dry sand, hauled myself over to the other side.

I reached the footpath and began the long slow walk over the golf course. People were passing to and fro asking if they could assist me at all. I obviously looked in a very bad way indeed. I thanked them for their concern, managed to find out where I was (Longniddry) and told them that I was meeting my wife. That was the plan anyway, although phone reception had become increasingly patchy so I wasn't entirely sure how much she had heard of my description of the current location.

On and on I walked. It seemed like forever, but I was learning a technique that minimised the pain a little. I found that if I could keep my left leg very straight when I put my foot on the ground then it didn't hurt too much. If my knee bent laterally at all then there were huge amounts of pain. Avoid that, I thought. It took massive amounts of concentration to keep that leg straight, and I could only take very tiny steps as I had to stop the knee attempting to bend at all.

My journey across the golf course was a very long trek indeed. At the other end I emerged onto another footpath and began limping up that one. Over a hedge I saw someone running. Carrie was there looking quite frantic. I yelled out that I was here and she did a kind of mad muppet flailing thing with her arms and whirled around to find her way back to the path that I was on. A couple of minutes later she found me and flung herself into my arms. It was very good to be reunited.

Carrie pointed me at the train station and we began our long slow walk up the hill. A very tall man appeared from nowhere and asked if we wanted a lift up to the train station. “Yes, absolutely!” yells I, “that would be brilliant.” He vanishes for several minutes and then reappears in a car and drives us to the train station. I think he must have seen us from his living room window and made the decision to help. Just a downright wonderful thing to do. Thank you, tall man from Longniddry. You are a damn fine chap.

The trains from Longniddry only run once every hour, so I had plenty of time to sit in the station feeling sorry for myself. Despite wanting to hide away, I still needed to make my way to the finish. I had put some warm clothes into a bag at the start and that bag was now waiting for me at the finish line in Musselburgh. We boarded the train and arrived in Musselburgh to find that the train station was nearly two miles away from Musselburgh town centre. How bizarre. Fortunately there was a bus and that took me within about a half mile of the finish.

Carrie and I limped along the high street but I was moving very slowly indeed. She decided to stash me in a Subway (where I bought a sandwich), take my number and go on to collect my bag. She also collected a friend of ours called Lynn, who had arranged to meet us at the finish line. They came back for me and we all went back to find another bus at my geologically slow limping speed. Back in Edinburgh there was a long slow trudge to Waverley station. At Waverley we caught a train to Ian and Elaine's house in Linlithgow. Then it was time to relax with ice on knee, raised foot, and beer. The physio hadn't mentioned anything about beer in her recommendations, but I'm sure that was just an oversight.

The beer was good, the knee pain was horrible, and the feeling of failure was almost overwhelming. However, I could take comfort from the fact that I had completed the London Marathon only a month before. I know I can run a marathon and I am sure that I will do again.

I will mend, but for now a poor broken marathon runner am I.

So that's my story. I am still trying to rehabilitate this knee. I am regularly doing my exercises, trying to strengthen the other muscles and pull the kneecap back into alignment. I have still only done one marathon but I'm sure there will be others.

I hope my tales of joy and woe have been of use to you, possibly in your own marathon attempts.

Save The Rhino

I discovered the charity Save The Rhino through the campaigning of the writer of *The Hitchhiker's Guide to the Galaxy*, Douglas Adams. Douglas was a founder patron and campaigned assiduously during his lifetime to raise the profile of the charity and so bring to the wider public the plight of the various rhino species.

It was in the early 1990s that the charity began to develop into a much more focussed organisation. The rise in rhino poaching had reached frightening levels as Dave Stirling and Johnny Roberts went on a 'rhino scramble' across Africa, raising money toward the fencing of the Aberdare Rhino Sanctuary. They made contacts with a large number of people who were doing incredible work to preserve the rhino species, including Rob Brett who was the Kenyan rhino programme coordinator at the time. This gave them lots of ideas about how to ensure that funds raised got to the places where they would be most useful, and infused them with huge amounts of enthusiasm.

The London Marathon was an obvious contender for fundraising opportunities and they enlisted as many friends as they possibly could to enter the marathon, raising money to send to the various rhino preservation projects taking place in Africa.

It was around this time that William Todd Jones made a phone call which resulted in finding himself at the centre of the fundraising shenanigans. Todd was a puppet designer and performer in an opera which had a bunch of dancing rhino. He offered the rhino costumes to the charity and his offer was enthusiastically accepted, with the added suggestion that he run the marathon with them while dressed in the costume. This was the start of something that has now become almost synonymous with the London Marathon. Whenever the subject of running the London Marathon in costume is mentioned, you can guarantee that at some point someone will say something about the rhino runners. The crowds absolutely adore the costumes – and the cheers, whistles and shouts of support when a rhino runner goes by is absolutely deafening.

Fundraising continued after the marathon with more runs, auctions, and that icon of the 1990s, the rave. All of this energy culminated in Save The Rhino becoming an official UK charity in 1994. It was in this year that Douglas Adams became involved with the organisation. He was giving a lecture at the Royal Geographical Society in London on his new book, *Last Chance To See*. Dave Stirling went along to see him and shortly afterwards Douglas became a founder patron of the charity. He also joined in with the wonderfully bizarre Mount Kilimanjaro climb, himself donning the costume for sections of the trek. Douglas wrote a little about the journey in his book *The Salmon of Doubt*. I love his description of the rhino costume:

"One of them is wearing a large, grey, sculptural edifice … A large horn bobs in front of it. The thing is a grotesque but oddly beautiful caricature of a rhinoceros moving along with swift, busy strides."

Save The Rhino still offer a 'climb Mount Kilimanjaro' experience for a fairly small registration fee and a pledge to raise funds for the charity (fortunately it is not obligatory to wear the rhino suit). Included in the Kilimanjaro experience is a visit to the Mikomazi Rhino Sanctuary. It really does look like an extraordinary opportunity. Take a look at the web page https://www.savetherhino.org/events/906_rhino_climb_kilimanjaro for more details. I must admit that I am awfully tempted myself. Maybe one day...

Save The Rhino continued to grow, getting involved in other crazy fundraising events such as running the gruelling Marathon De Sables (251 kilometres of Saharan desert) in rhino costume, more auctions, more parties, and – after the sad death of Douglas Adams – the yearly memorial lecture at the Royal Geographical Society.

Save The Rhino International has now grown from raising around £300,000 in the year 2000 to having raised £1,300,000 in 2014-15. It is still quite a small charity compared to many, but it has a huge reach and manages to focus all money raised very tightly on areas where it is most needed. It is faced with an uphill struggle as the belief that rhino horn has magical medicinal properties goes back many thousands of years. The sums of money paid for horns in countries such as China and Vietnam is truly astounding, and the trade will continue to flourish as long as the mistaken belief that rhino horn (which is just keratin, the same material as your hair and nails are made from) can cure all ills from fever to cancer.

Save The Rhino target their resources on education, on lobbying governments, and on rhino sanctuaries, guards and breeding programmes to try to change minds and to preserve the few creatures that are left. It can look hopeless, especially with examples such as the Northern White Rhino of which, in 2016, there are only three left in the entire world (that's not a misprint: there actually are only three). However, not all is doom and gloom: a different sub-species, the Southern White Rhino, is actually increasing in population. We can make a difference for the rhino.

I suspect it can often feel disheartening for people associated with Save The Rhino. The situation for rhino all over Africa is incredibly desperate . Rangers risk their lives daily trying to protect them from the continuous encroachment of poachers and unfortunately several rangers have been killed.

Despite all of this, Save The Rhino manages to maintain a very playful approach to fundraising. I feel that this is important, lest we are crushed under the weight of despair. Serious frowns and internal angst aren't likely to help the rhinos one jot when we're fundraising. Yes, it is heartbreaking when we see more pictures of rhino slaughtered by poachers, but please try to remain upbeat and join in with whatever fun and games Save The Rhino may get up to.

If you've bought this book (rather than stolen it from that poor unfortunate person who fell asleep next to you on the train) then you have already donated to Save The

Rhino International. I hope you will donate again, either by buying multiple copies of this book (and maybe building a fort with them or creating a very large single book library on your Kindle, if you've bought an ebook), or logging on to the Save The Rhino website https://www.savetherhino.org/ and donating there.

Made in the USA
Columbia, SC
20 April 2017